29 Monster Real Estate Agents' Scripts & Tips

By: Bob Bloom

Copyright
Case #1-4965806751
Date 4/24/2017

Dedicated to my 29 Monsters
Thank you for sharing.

Table of Contents

1st Question to Ask a Prospect	1
Buyers Script/ Early On	7
Buyer Scripts/ Closing	10
The Mr. Mellow Close	14
Buyer Scripts/ Making the Offer	16
Buyer Scripts/ Counter Offer	24
Buyer Scripts/ Dad Look 1st	30
Buyer Scripts/ Random Thoughts	32
Seller Scripts/ Presenting the Offer	34
Seller Scripts/ Price Reduction	43
Seller Scripts/ Reduce Commission	47
Seller Scripts/ Friend in Business	53

Seller Scripts/ Random Thoughts	57
Referral Scripts	62
Referral Transition Scripts	71
Affirmations on Steroids	74
Affirmations for Referrals	82
Affirmations for Closing	85
2nd Best Database	88
Great Referral Sources	91
New Words=New Results	95
To Phone or Not to Phone	98
Quitters Prosper	99
The Price is Right Game	106
Farming	109
The Bond Market	115
Expireds for Wimps	118
Fastest Niche Development	120
U.S.P.S./ Me.S.P.S.	124

8X8	126
3 Rituals for Success	130
Hello I am a Realtor	136
You are NOT a Realtor	138
Weekly Goals	143
Trivia Quiz	148
Big Groups=Big Bucks	153
Coming Soon	157
A Story of 2 Agents	159
Tell 'em You're Great	161
Teams; When & Why	164
Teams Common Mistakes	168
Database Building Tip	171
Segmentation	175
Don't Worry Be Happy	183
Welcome	185

Zillow	189
Luxury Homes	193
Be Like the Salmon	200
Snow Day	201
Prospecting 101	206
Baseball's Greatest	210
Pain or Pleasure	212
Combo Bombo to Success	217
The Fast Eat the Slow	223
Now You See it….	225
Normal Market Tip	229
Warren Says	231
Same Words but Why	233
Reticular Activator	240
2 Most Important Questions	243

My first year in the real estate business, I was a Monster. It was the late 70's and a much different profession. I worked FSBO's, landed my first builder and really focused. I had a blast. I was a Monster and had an annual sales volume that first year of 2.5 million dollars.

I could start this book from many directions. Starting at the fact that there was a time when 2.5 million made me a Monster, says it all. The business model has changed dramatically. That was a time when we had an industry award we called the "Million Dollar Club." Few of us attained it and if we did, it went on the business card. It was something to be proud of. Today, you may reach that volume as the co-listing agent on one Luxury Listing.

That first year I was taught to get a shoebox and keep 3x5 cards in it with my clients' names and info. It was suggested that I arrange the files by phone number because?????

We did not have databases, individual brands or any concept of how to build a business. No one had an assistant. What we did have was "The Book." All of the listings came out on Tuesday in a book. This huge book was dropped off at midnight and "WE" had the book. We could not share the book with our clients. That is what made us valuable. Without me, they had no information.

It was a bit like "Ralph has the conch…"

Re/Max was the first big thing to come along. Before that, Monster agents would secretly negotiate our "Split". I got up to 70% if I promised not to tell anyone. Many agents had a 50/50 split their whole career. When the Monsters learned they could pay RE/Max a desk fee and keep their own money….. it changed everything.

There was now a real incentive for forward thinkers to develop their own business model, within the real estate sales context.

As they did, Gary Keller found them. Keller sought out the Monsters around the country and shared with all of us, what they had done to become one. In his book, The Millionaire Real Estate Agent, Keller taught us all how to run a business instead of sell houses.

Now there are Monsters everywhere. Every community has some real estate agents that are running a business. The old 80/20 rule, no longer applies. In most communities, the Monsters are tipping the scales. The ratio is 90/10 in many MLS groups.

There are new business models and strategies that are already proven. It no longer means that you are a great salesperson if you are a Monster. You are probably a great businessperson and are running your business, as one.

I love how the best of the best, in our industry are so willing to share. They do not feel threatened. There is plenty for others. Most of them modeled another and they now wish you well.

Though there were some interesting differences in their game plan, they had much in common. They shared with an open heart to me. I hope to do the same with you. The point of this book is not for you to be a Monster. Be one if you choose.

The point is to share some strategies the Monsters use and see if some version of that, would improve your life. The goal is to continue on the path of improvement. Here are a few ways others have done so.

This book is for real estate agents. I am both a real estate agent and a Realtor. Sometimes in this book I use the terms almost interchangeably. They are not. "Realtor" is a registered trademark of the National Association of Realtors. All Realtors prescribe to certain ethical standards that all real estate agents, do not. I use the term as one of respect and believe all of us agents should belong to our association. They do much good or us on the political front and attempt to keep up our ethical treatment towards each other and our perception with the public.

1st Question to Ask a Prospect

We are all aware of the importance of the infamous, "First Impression." How important it is, to immediately leave a favorable impression, with our potential client, or our fate may be sealed, before we open our mouth.

To add extra pressure to that moment, I would like to add, that the success of your entire relationship with this person, could actually revolve around their answer to your initial question. The subtleties of their answering process, tell it all.

Tell it all that is, if you ask the right question. Ask the wrong question and the opportunity is lost. The art of "Question #1," separates the winners from the losers. Start with something like, "Nice to meet you sir. How are you?"… and as the chant goes…. It's all over….

O.K. That might be a bit dramatic. However, you have the ability to gain the upper hand right from the beginning.

The first question is vitally important. I suggest you go with something like: "When you were a kid, what color, was your favorite lunchbox?" A classic. Or perhaps, your style leans towards: "What is your 3rd and 4th favorite, type of dog?" I love that one and it is quite effective, though I personally lean towards the lunchbox query.

Steal my ideas and tweak my words. Make them your own. You might choose a different question to start the conversation with, but do not stray far. What do these two queries have in common? They are not easily answered, without taking a moment to remember back and recall. It requires the prospect, to think and not just answer with something, that is on the tip of their tongue. Ask their favorite color and they respond blue, without thinking.

1st Question

Asking their 3rd favorite color requires thought, before responding.

That is the key. When they need to think back before answering your question, they reveal to you, their thinking style.

They do that with their eyes.

There are 3 major thinking styles. One is not better than the other. We just use the one that is our instinctively natural way, to look at things. You care, because you will be much more successful, if you match your presentation and words, to fit how your prospect easily digests information. If we present our story, in a different thinking style, they need to stop and convert it, to what makes sense to them. It does not flow for them as well, as if we made it easy and comfortable for them.

The three thinking styles are:
Visual
Kinesthetic
Digital

When you ask them a thought-provoking question, they will show you which thinking style they use, with their eyes.

Visual

People that are visual, "see" the situation. When they recall, they remember and see a video, of the event. When they buy a house, they want a view. You would stand on the deck with this buyer. They are more likely to want lots of windows, open spaces with a vaulted ceiling, new cabinets in the kitchen and a view of some sort.

You would be wise to have professional looking presentation sheets that you can pull out as needed. If you have a colorful chart to make your point, they really will stop and look at it. They are visual, so slow down and let them see. Let them slowly see the pretty chart and stand still when you are on the deck. Do not look at the yard and then head back inside. Go slow everywhere there is a visual component to the home. Let them visually enjoy the experience.

When you are finished showing them the home, take them back to the best view, to visit.

You are wise to use words such as: "How does this look to you?" and "How do you see this home?" or "Is there anything I else I can show you" or "Before we go would you like to see the deck again?"

. When you ask the big, thought provoking question of someone, who has a predominantly, visual" thinking style, they pause and look up, to recall the answer. Watch their eyes. They look up, usually off to the right or left, but always up.

1st Question

Kinesthetic

People that are kinesthetic, "feel" the situation. When they recall, they remember, how the event felt. When they buy a house, they feel the family room's fireplace coziness and how it feels to bring family together around the kitchen nook. They are more likely to prefer warm colors that make them feel a certain way.

Talk to them about family gatherings and ask if certain rooms would work for that. Listen and watch closely. If they find a room that feels cozy to them, spend extra time there.

It is important to use a kinesthetic's comfort words. Use the same words that are in their normal vocabulary. Do not overwhelm them with repetitive data. It needs to feel right for this "kinesthetic" thinker.

You might choose to use words such as: "How does this home feel to you?" or "Would you like to share your feelings about…?" or "Are you comfortable with this house?" or "How do you feel about making an offer?"

When you ask the big, thought provoking, question, of someone who has a predominantly, "kinesthetic" thinking style, they pause and look down, to remember how that event felt. It is usually off to the right or left as well, but always down. Watch their eyes. They look down before they answer the tough question.

Digital

People that are digital, "analyze" the situation. When they make a recollection, or make a decision, they analyze the facts of the event. When they buy a house, it needs it to make sense. You stress the neighborhood values, ease of re-sell, monthly payment after tax write-off, kids each getting their own bedroom and drive time to school or work. Not necessarily fun to work with a digital client because they are looking for a bargain or may buy nothing.

Reassure them that the purchase is wise. If their spouse is visual, talk about how a home with a view is a good investment and worth more than one without a view. Do not bore them with graphs and charts but they will internalize facts so do show those. They want all the data available. Nothing more exciting than a septic inspection report to this person.

It needs to make sense, to the "digital" buyer. They are very logical and need their questions answered, so they can check each question off the list, before they move on. Do every bit of follow-up that you commit to. Find ways to provide value by providing more data than you might for other buyers.

When you ask the big, thought provoking question, of someone who has a predominantly "digital" thinking style, they pause and look sideways to recall or think through the response. It might be right or left but they will look sideways.

1st Question

We all have some of all three styles, in us and we use all three styles of thinking, to make major decisions. Do not insult the kinesthetic buyer, by ignoring the facts or not using visuals. We are best, when we have satisfied all three styles, of our client. Just understand, that one style is dominant and their "go to" process, for making decisions. After the kinesthetic thinks it looks OK and the numbers check, back to: "This just feels right."

This is your first script. Do this at the first appointment. Look for reasons to interject a question, that requires thought and watch carefully. That allows you, from the very beginning, to break through a few feet of the ice. If you can figure out early on, how to tweak your presentation and your words and your style, to be in their dominant language……

Boomshackalacka….

Buyer scripts
Early On

Early on with a buyer that was from a cold source

"The majority of my business comes from my old clients and the people they refer to me. As a result, meeting you is a bit rare for me and I am so glad we did. You seem like (a real nice person, a very logical person, an open and honest person....) and I am honored to help you if I can?

I just have two requests. One: if I am doing a good job that you use me as your agent when we find a good property. Is that one OK? And two: if at any time you are **not happy** with my efforts that you let me know. All right?

Early on with a buyer that was referred to me

The vast majority of my business comes from my past clients or people they refer to me. Like in your case. I sure enjoyed working with so and so. She said we would get along great.

When I help people I have 3 requests:
 1st when we find a home, I am your Realtor

 2nd if you are ever unhappy, tell me and I will release you from #1. But you have to tell me.

 3rd if I do a good job you will consider referring your friends to me when they need to move.

Are you OK with that?

Early on with a new buyer 8

Thought I should cover with you, how I work. I will be totally committed to helping you get to the best property out there. I don't care which one pays me a higher fee or even if it is a "for sale by owner" that decides to not pay me a fee. I will work for free if we get you the best house.

But here's my deal. I want the same commitment from you. As we chase around properties, you need to tell the Realtor at the open house you stop by or the agent that answers the phone from the number on a for sale sign, that you have a Realtor but wanted some information. We get those calls all the time and are thrilled to promote our listings to any buyer. We of course will try and get any new buyer that calls but if they have an agent we are still thrilled to help them.

Same with "for sale by owners" I don't have time to chase them all. If you spot one forward the info to me. Here's the deal with the For sale By Owners. My experience is that they have no clue what to do when they get a buyer. They are thrilled to throw me a reduced fee to help them out. Some of them, will not pay a nickel. By God they don't need no stinking Realtor.

Well, you do. If you run across any FSBO don't you dare sign legal documents without being represented. If it ends up the perfect house for you is a For Sale By Owner that won't pay me a fee, so be it. Keep me involved. It is very important.

Prepare them to refer

I'd like to take a minute to tell you how I work. The majority of my business comes from referrals from my past clients. When that happens, it is as if I almost have 2 clients,

You, my primary client & the person that referred you to me. I feel like I have a responsibility to them to do a great job for you so that they are glad they did that.

29 Monsters

Because most of my business is referral, I don't spend so much time out chasing around potential clients. It frees me up to focus on whom I am currently working with. I would like to ask that if that if you are also happy with my efforts, that you consider doing the same? As you bump into somebody that is considering a move, my hope is that would you introduce them to me? That allows me to spend my time searching for the right home for you. Will you do that?

Buyer Scripts
Closing

Just a quick thought on closing….We don't close on people thinking some new technique will get people to buy a house they don't want. That ain't gonna happen… We still have to get through the long process to closing and if they are not committed… it ain't gonna happen.

The reason we practice our buyer closing scripts, is because it is so very sad that over and over people lose out on their 1st choice home. Their lack of decision making ability, freezes them into inaction. It is so sad.

We do not have closing scripts to trick people and get a commission. We have closing scripts so that we can do our jobs, be a professional and "help" the people we represent. Then we can sleep at night. Close or insomnia for you.

I believe that any agent that proudly announces that they are not a high pressure sales person and don't close, should lose their license. Seriously. You have an obligation as a professional to close on your buyers. If you do not, hand in the license. You don't deserve one.

When you first met your client you promised that you would help them. You said how hard you would work and really try to help them get the perfect house. If at the time they need your help the most, you fail, you should lose your license. We are supposed to help them BUY a home. Not show them homes.

Do not call yourself a professional if you are not a closer. You are not.

It is difficult for many people to make a decision. Their grandpa told them to always go home and sleep on it and they love their gramps. Their mama told them to be wary of sales folks and you are one. They seldom need to make huge decisions in their everyday life and are nervous to make a mistake. They do not realize that hesitation is a bigger risk than making a quick and thus poor, decision. In real estate you can always get out of quick and thus bad, decisions. There are plenty of legal outs. You can never recapture the missed opportunity of indecision. If your client misses out it is your fault that you didn't care enough to at least try and close them twice.

You said you would help. Help them. Close them. They hired you to get 'er done and get them moved. They did not choose you because you have a lockbox key and can show them homes. They asked you to help them **buy** a home not look at homes. You are the professional. Help them to move in to this fabulous home.

Any uncomfortableness that comes with a closing situation is way, way, way offset by the joyful celebration of home ownership. Booyah... Experience a dash of discomfort and way more joy. Cool. Close them.

If you only close once or you let them offer too low without trying to help them, you are unprofessional and narcissistic. Yes, self centered, to have some hang up where you don't give people a second chance to talk through their emotions and make the right decision. Not everyone just folds and says thank you are right after the first close. They need to work through it. Your most appreciative and loyal clients will be those that you helped overcome their fear. They may not verbalize it but they know you helped them to not be a chicken. You made them look good and they love their home. The home they might not own if you hadn't helped them. Cool....

The decision that you know they should make, you usually know before they do. If it is the right home, help them. It is not OK to be so mellow that your client misses out on a great home. If you won't do it, move aside so someone can help them and not break their heart.

Buyer Scripts/Closing

You can't close on people until they find the right house. In order to know if you are in the right house, you need to know what they want.

As you show them houses ask, does this dining room fit your furniture or do you have a hutch. What furniture do you have for your master bedroom? Look @ walls together to decide if there is room etc. With each room slowly gather the data to know which home fits their needs.

We do not close until we are helping them buy the right home. That is what gives us the confidence to feel good about adding some pressure. You are pretty darn sure that you are doing them a huge favor. You are helping them…. Some say closing….

Close set-up

When you know that you are in the right home for your client, give the buyer time to absorb that. Try stepping out on the deck or in another room, where you can still be heard by the buyers and call the listing agent. Get the scoop on the home while they can hear you. It gives them some time to talk without you, let's them see that you are a person of action and it shows urgency. When you saw that the home was a good one, you acted. That encourages them to understand that action is required on this one. Old Bob didn't call on every home just this one, which is a really good one. Bob knew we might need to act fast on this one.

You also build credibility when they hear you talk professionally to the other agent while clearly representing them.

If you are lucky enough that the other real estate agent told you a reason to close them, close them. Tell them there is activity or another offer coming or whatever is true. They know you are speaking from truth and not salesmanship. They heard the call. Close them.

Sometimes the listing agent gives us the seller's hot button, if we ask. Tell your buyers that as a negotiation point, the listing agent tells me that it is important for the seller if…. Blah… blah… blah… Most of our competition that are going to write an offer, won't know that. It gives us an advantage if we can work around that. Are you OK with renting back to the seller for up to 30 days? (or whatever is something you heard that sets you apart, besides price) Perfect. Let's write that in and then we can show the seller that we are trying to be the perfect buyer for them. It should help us a little, if there are other offers."

Pseudo Closes

Would you like to sit down and see what the paperwork looks like on this home?
Do I sense that this home is pretty darn close.
How do you feel about this home?
Could you see your family living here?
Do you need to see any part of the home again while we are here?
So, is this the Smith family home?
If we are going to look at the paperwork we should sit right here since the seller is gone.
Would your family feel comfortable here?

Visual Clients:
　　Can you see yourself living here?

Kinesthetic Clients:
　　How does this home feel to you?

Digital buyers:
　　Does this home make sense to you?

The Mr. Mellow Close

As salespeople, some of us resist doing our jobs. Our job is to get people moved and that requires closing the prospect, to get an agreement.

I hear all kinds of excuses for weak and ineffective sales folks, that don't close. I hear:

--- I'm not high pressure
--- I don't want to make them feel uncomfortable
--- They should go home and think about it
--- I work with friends and family
--- I hate to be sold so I know they won't either

There is no excuse, for not closing. If you care about the buyer and you have the right proposal, you are a jerk, if you don't help them buy. It is difficult for many people to make a decision. They were taught to be careful and beware salesmen. Great grandpa told them to always go home and sleep on it and they loved their gramps. If you said you would help them, help them. When they are on the edge but need help to get over it, push them.

Buyers and sellers respect and want to work with strong sales people. They appreciate confidence and enthusiasm. They are not inspired to buy, if the real estate agent isn't inspired enough by this property, to get excited and try to close.

If you are easing into the world of closing, here is a start. Dip your toes into the rich waters, with my Mr. Mellow Close.

29 Monsters

John, I have to tell you something. One of my weaknesses as a salesman, is I'm a lousy salesman. Really, I want to be better, but I am just not good at the whole "Closing" thing.

Every year, I have a few clients, who miss out on a great house because I was too mellow to tell them, "You know, we should probably do this." They sleep on it and when they call me back and say, "We love it. This would be great." it's too late and they miss out. Then I feel terrible. I am trying to be respectful and not pressure people, but sometimes, because I am Mr. Mellow, my client misses out.

I happen to like you and I want to do my job well for you. Does this happen to be one of those situations where I am supposed to help you, buy this?

Making the Offer 16

Buyer scripts
Making the Offer

You will think that I am lying. You will think I am making this up for dramatic effect. You would be wrong. I actually know more than one real estate agent that when it is the obvious time to write an offer, they lead with "How much do you want to offer?"

I was considering naming this chapter "DUH!" One of the reasons we have scripts is because we are supposed to help **lead people BEFORE** they say something stupid. Whatever number falls out of their mouth, becomes a number they dig their heels in to defend. Stop them before they make that mistake. It is a cheap shot for you to not take control here and help them.

We don't ask what do they **WANT** to offer. Duh, they want to offer a hundred dollars and steal it. They have watched all the reality real estate shows and they too want to get the best home in the county at a stupid cheap price. That is what they **want to offer.**

Our job is to help people. With all of the scripts, we need to keep that in mind. If this is the best house for your client and they want it, don't let their ignorance of the market or of how buying a home works, from them getting their dream home. If they say a price in response to your query that is the number they will defend. You asked them. They answered.

I recommend you develop a script that follows the following steps:

Stop them
Story
Seller view
Not a Negotiating Moment
Be 1st

Stop them

It is important to lead your client before they decide a price to offer. When you are sitting down take control before they do.

If they blurt out a number before you can stop them, take a long thoughtful pause. Do not respond right away. Let them feel that you are hesitating about that number even though you aren't arguing about it. Then proceed onto the next step of "Story."

Story

Before you talk price, tell them a story.
It might be similar to:

"OK guys, so this is a pretty fabulous home and I am not surprised if this is the one you want to live in. I bet we both knew it the minute we walked in.

OR....

"Wow, this is a pretty great property. Besides having all the amenities that you are looking for it also has R.V. Parking (or a corner lot or a view or a shed or nice trees or school district or…or.. or…) Because of that, this home is going to be a hot one. The buyers that need that R.V. parking will pay extra to get it because there are so few that have that and are still this nice. Now I realize that may not have value for you now but when you sell, it will., This is a great one that met all your needs, plus RV parking. Somebody is going to love this.

Making the Offer 18

OR…..

" I don't have to tell you guys how hot this house is going to be. We have made enough offers to know that.

OR….

I talked to the listing agent and they are getting a lot of activity already. There are a couple agents that are setting up a second showing. I am so glad we got in to see this one on time before all the bidding war begins. Hopefully."

OR….

I have to tell you, I've done this long enough to know that when we see this many business cards this soon, it is about to sell. Apparently we are not the only one that wants to buy the **nicest home in the $X price range, because this is a nice home.**

Seller view

It helps our buyers be more realistic if we can get them to pause for a moment and consider what the seller might be thinking. Make the seller a human not an anonymous opponent. They are people and have all the same data that you have. They too know how to go online and probably also watch the news. If the market is hot, they too know it.

Consider:
"As you can imagine the seller must be feeling pretty cocky right now."

OR...

This appears to be a pretty savvy seller. I bet she knows what she has here yet has it priced to get a lot of activity. Probably hoping for a bidding war."

OR...

"I know this listing agent. He/she is pretty good. I am positive that agent has shown the seller all the comps and knows they have s good one here. We are not going to sneak up on a stupid seller on this one.

Not a Negotiating Moment

Your client's goal is to get a great house. The media has confused them into thinking that lots of people get a great steal if they offer low enough. They think that is the goal. To steal a great home. It is not nor is it reasonable to think that. If they do indeed think that way, it is your fault. Deal with the false expectations or find a different client.

We need to encourage them to remember the goal. Home Sweet Home.

Making the Offer 20

Try words similar to:

"The goal is to respond quicker than our competition not to think we are Donald Trump, right? If we want this one, we probably need to decide fairly quickly and just buy it because this is a good one. The goal with this house might be to just plain be first."

OR...

You know my job isn't as fun in this market. A few years ago we could have had a riot strategizing how we best great a buy. Now my job seems to be one of who is fastest. It looks to me like this is one of those situations where the quickest person that gives them what they want, gets it."

OR...

"Guys this next part is the hardest part of the whole process and where many buyers blow it. Sometimes when we feel we are educated on the market and a really good house comes up, we just need to buy it. I know that the T.V. shows tell you to try some silly low offer but in my world in this county and at this price range, we might just say please and thank you."

OR...

"Guys, you need to understand something. I am not some high-pressure salesman that has the big close coming now that we probably found the right house. You are going to have to speak up. A house like this goes quickly usually, so you need to be able to tell me to pull the trigger if this is the right one." If they say nothing say "Is this the right one?"

Be 1ˢᵗ

In the current real estate market that I am in, it is pretty hot. Since I first got my real estate license in 1978, I have seen both good and bad markets. I understand that sometimes in buyer markets that we would not do ourselves a favor by being quick. The sellers needed some time to get depressed awhile first. However, waiting for that moment usually meant that someone else came in and found the sellers bottom dollar.

I submit that almost always being first is an advantage and a must in a seller's market.

Try"

"As the Realtor in the room I believe I am supposed to encourage to move quickly if you want this home."

OR...

"After all the houses we have seen, I think the goal with this one is to be first."

OR...

"This is not being high pressure but you hired me to help you and I think we need to really try and be the first one to offer on this home. It will not last long."

Or...

"We might get lucky and avoid a bidding war if we move fast enough."

Making the Offer

If they choose to offer low anyway try:

After years of experience (or if you are new, talking to the best agents) I found that homes almost always sell for market value. If we offer below that value, we usually won't get it.

OR...

We've seen a lot of houses will you be disappointed if you don't get this home?

OR...

I represent you and will always do as you wish. However, I think it is my job to say something here. Is that OK?

Every year I have a few clients that miss out on what ended up being the best home for their needs and budget because they were just a little bit apart on price. If this is a home that you would love for years, I am supposed to make sure you stop once more and ponder that. This is not a commission thing. This is me doing my job and saying this might be your house and if it is, don't miss it. (or blow it)

OR...

I understand that you want to offer low and because I represent you I will do whatever you choose. However, it is my job to pause a moment. Every year I have clients lose out on their dream house because they offered too low instead of moving toward ...(describe their dream of country or bigger or smaller or...)

I am guessing this seller is a human and those darn humans are sooo unpredictable. I can't pretend I know how they will respond. I do know they would accept $X. Sometimes the whole negotiation thing ends up not as good as we hoped for, if we tick off the seller of the home we want to buy.

Buyer Scripts
Counter Offer

An interesting thing often happens after an offer is made. Many buyers get nervous that they won't get the home and start to wish they had offered higher. That is especially true if the offer can not be presented the same day and the potential buyer has a chance to sleep on it.

I say that because many agents have a tendency to think their buyer will be locked in to their offering price. They take negative vibes with them when they present the counter. They are assuming that the buyer will not budge. Sometimes they think that because their buyer used words like "I won't budge."

Ignore them. When you return with the counter pretend you don't know that they took such a hard stance. Start anew. There is a good chance that they have softened so DO NOT take them back to that assumption. Ignore it. That gives them an out. If you re-mention their earlier stance they are more likely to defend it again. Help them to save face and move on.

I recommend a 5-step presentation. Make your script follow the flow of the following:

Pause & Be Thoughtful
Transition
Dream
Problem
Good News

Pause & Be Thoughtful

It is easy for us to reek of commission need at this appointment. Often the buyer feels we are selling them to accept something which was different than what they wanted. When that happens, the trust factor is reduced and we are no longer in a position to have our thoughts heard by our buyer.

Pausing, lets the buyer know that we are contemplating and not just selling. It is important to go slow. We can easily ramp up a bit when we smell a sale. Don't do that in the counter presentation. Go slow and listen to their words.

Transition

When I need to go back to the buyer with a counter offer, I try to not just lead with price. They know it isn't good but help them to soften before you give the bad news. Try:

Well guys, we did pretty good but we did not get the price we had hoped for.

OR...

"We knew this was a good one and we were right. The seller is getting a lot of activity and is not too worried about selling at that price."

OR...

I think it is my job as the Realtor in the room to say something. Is that OK?

OR...

One of the reasons you hired me was for my negotiation skills. I didn't succeed with the seller but this is important to me to get you into this home. I think that I am supposed to ask you to approach this with an open mind if I am doing my job."

OR...

My job is to pause here for a moment ... We have looked at a lot of homes and this is one of the best.

Dream

Remind them of their dream. Why is it that this was the right home? Try something similar to:

"I have to tell you. We looked at a lot of homes and this one came closest to fitting your needs."

OR...

"I know this process is stressful but I am so glad we have at least had the opportunity to negotiate on a home that had the yard that you hoped for."

OR...

"This would be easier for me to give you the news of a counter offer if I didn't know how well this home fits your needs. I have to say as a Realtor I am nervous that I won't find this home again."

OR...

"I know you guys really want this home and that we probably won't find that nice of a master bedroom again, so please I am trying to do my best. Apparently lots of buyers love that master bedroom."

Problem

State the problem. Let them know there is an obstacle that can not be overcome. Try:

"The problem guys, is that the seller knows what he has here. He has seen the comps and is very cocky that the home is priced fair."

OR...

"The problem is that they are getting a lot of activity and expect more offers soon."

OR...

"The problem is that the seller has already found the home they want and this counter represents the lowest price they can accept and still make that move.

Buyer Counter

OR...

"The problem is that the house up the street just sold for this price and is not as nice as this home. This might be a pretty good value compared to that comp."

OR...

"I have to tell you something. Sometimes I am too mellow to do some big closing thing. I respect my clients and don't want to pressure them. However because of that, every year some client of mine misses out on the right house because I am too mellow. This is a fabulous house and I can't let this be one of those times."

Good News

We need to people to feel good about their decisions. We need to bring their state of mind back to that happy place they were in when they made the offer. Always end with "Guys here is the good news." Add to that something like:

"The house is yours if you want it and move quickly."

OR...

"We have found the seller's bottom price without making them angry. Nicely done. Now it is yours if you want it."

OR...

"The ball is in your court. This is the best home we found that met your needs. You are in control of whether or not you move there. We now have the seller's best price."

29 Monsters

OR...

"There are no other offers written yet. If you decide to accept this we can get it off the market before that happens. As soon as you sign this I can transmit a copy to the other real estate agent and then the seller is stuck with us."

OR...

""The ball is in your court. You can afford this home if you want it and I believe we found the lowest price possible."

OR...

"You can afford this home if you choose. It fits your needs better than any other home we saw and this is a fair price. It isn't as low as you'd like but you are still getting a fair value on your 1st choice (or a fabulous) home.

OR...

"It's interesting to me. After doing this for years (or talking to the best agents that have done this for years) I find that the best homes almost always sell for market value. It is the distressed and less desirable homes that people get a bit lower price. It's amazing but the best ones, end up selling for market value.

Buyer scripts

When dad is going to come take a look

My favorite words as a Realtor have always been, "We like the home a lot but we need to have dad come take a look first." Aye Yi Yi... daaaaaaad....

This is the same dad that paid $28,500 for his home on an acre, about 50 years ago. The same dad that never moved because he didn't have the nerve, to pull the trigger a couple of times. The same dad who feels he is being called in to protect his kid from some slick salesman.

It can go either way when old dad comes but the risk is always great. Poor dad. It is a lose/lose proposition. We are walking a tight rope when we respond to that statement. Do not put the buyer in a defensive mode by mocking that she wants the one person she trusts the most, to come look.

Keep the buyer educated. Prepare them for the inevitable. If they are prepared ahead of time they will be better able to respond appropriately. I might say something like:

"I have to tell you something, so you know. I am a dad and would really love to be part of my daughters.. anything...especially buying a home. Because of that I have a special place in my heart, when in situations like this, dad (or uncle or...) cares enough to come out. It is pretty cool. You are lucky to have that relationship.

But I have to tell you something and it might not apply in your case. There is **a lot of pressure** on "so and so" when he comes out here to protect you. That's why they are coming. To protect you. And the hardest part is that often this person hasn't bought a home in a long time. They don't know the market, near as well as you do. You know they didn't see (name the worst home you showed them or a couple of bad ones if you can) They have a lot of pressure on them if you buy it and then the roof caves in… I tell you this so you are aware, that I tend to be very patient with good people that care about a nice person like you. Just know we might both just **have to be a bit patient.** I want to hear their thoughts but I totally get the tough lose/lose spot they are in. I promise I won't say anything when he suggests we offer $29,000.

    I literally have clients wink at me when dad starts to go off, on how expensive the home is. If I hadn't prepared them they might have been gotten scared. I gave them the confidence to know, that "they" know the current real estate market better than the advisor.

Buyer scripts
Random Thoughts

While showing property
After 2nd home. Which of those 2 was your favorite.
After 3rd home. Did you like it better than the current #1?

What do you like about this house?

Do I sense that this home is pretty darn close.

How do you feel about this home?

Could you see your family living here?

Do you need to see any part of the home again while we are here?

So, is this the Smith family home?

Second close (or need to think about it or sleep on it)
Only if you know that you have the right house for the buyer and they are just afraid to pull the trigger, try this:

"I am here to protect you so I want you to know that I have built in a legal out. If you go home and change your mind, you don't have to be up all night worrying. If you want out in the morning, just give me a call and you're out. I think the important thing about **this home** is that if you have some pretty good interest, we need to tie it up and get it off the market, right now. Right now. This one will go soon. Let's tie it up and then you can take a breath and make sure it is right. This is not a pressure salesman thing, because I am coaching you how to back out in the morning. This is an old Bob (old pro, friend, agent that cares) thing because every year some of my buyers lose their 1st choice home by waiting over night to write the offer. If this is probably the right home, we need to go now. I've got your back."

Wrap up

After you write the offer make them feel good about their decision. Reduce buyer's remorse by solidifying their decision, in their mind. Try:

I really like this home because it fits your needs. I love the... (restate their favorite feature of the home) so much But also, I know someday in about a million years you are going to call me to help you move again and this home will always be a great listing. I don't care how long you live here, this is a great investment. When you want to sell, someone will love the "X" feature just like you do. Nicely done.

Seller Offer

Seller
Presenting the Offer

How the offer is presented matters. The order, in which we use our words, matters. Whenever we talk about scripts, we start with the steps. The process is most important and then we find the words. I believe a good process for presenting an offer is:

Stop from discussing price
Pause
Acknowledge
Transition
Story
Close

Stop from saying price

I am not being cute with you. We can not avoid talking about the sales price right away or we will frustrate our client. We represent them and if we do some cutesy thing where we talk about what a great closing date and they don't want the swing set, instead of price, our clients lose trust in us.

29 Monsters

If the price is low, acknowledge it but do not allow a conversation to open about it. Shut that down. You can tell them the price and let them know that the price is lower than either of you hoped and you are going to need a conversation about that. But first, I want you to see the rest of the details of the offer and then I promise you I want to come back and talk about price. STOP the conversation from happening right then.

Above all else do not let the seller mention a counter price. Try to lead your seller before they make a statement, as to how they want to counter. Just as with a buyer, once someone has openly stated what they want to offer or counter offer, they feel the need to defend it. When people respond quickly, it is always from an emotional standpoint. We need to stop that before it happens. Save your clients from themselves. If they say something stupid, they might be stuck with it. Let them know that it is important to you to talk about price but hold off just a second.

We do that for a couple reasons:

First: we throw them back in to their logical brain use, when we start talking details of the transaction. It forces them out of their emotional brain side and forces them to look at logical things. Possession, does the refrigerator stay or go, inspection details, financing contingency.... Are all logical things to discuss, logically. Price is emotional. Reduce the emotion before you go back to visit price.

Second: we need to lead then through a story before they decide. We need to help them relax and understand the buyer is not a professional negotiator. Help your seller understand what buyers are thinking and that they are just humans doing what you're trying to do. They too are scared and nervous and don't want to be stupid.

Seller Offer

When you take control and avoid the seller saying a counter price, you are helping them immensely. They have seen all the TV shows and they want to be smart. They know the buyers are sharks and they are all secret flippers. Oh no, they want to flip this house. Well, maybe. Help them relax and see the bigger picture. They are not on TV and we have a real buyer that likes your home and wants to raise a family or a garden or something.

Make the negotiating gap smaller, by leading them, before they respond on price.

Pause

I talk about pausing many places. This is definitely one of them. You are trying to defuse stress and emotion. After you go through the offer tell them you'd like to talk about price now? Then pause. You are not building trust if you immediately deliver a polished "hammer the seller" close. They do not feel you are on their side, if you give a quick and thus canned, response. Then they must battle both you and the buyer. The pause let's them see you are reflecting on their particular situation. It shows you care enough to be thoughtful in your answers. They feel like a client receiving advice instead of a potential sale.

Really. Pause and reflect. When you start speaking, do so slowly and thoughtfully. If you are visiting with someone who you know will never sit still through a pause, say, "It is important that we get back to the price concern now. Since I am the Realtor may I go first?" If they say yes, then take your pause.

Let them know you did not go first to pound them. You are going first because it is your job and you are thinking about how best to express yourself. You are thinking about that because you care and want to represent them well.

Acknowledge

Do not pretend that it is no big deal. When it is their money, it is a big deal. You must acknowledge that you understand that. You are on their team. Their team had hoped for a higher price. You can say just that.

"I know WE hoped for more."

OR...

"This looks like a strong buyer but I know this is not the price we originally had in mind."

OR...

Look guys, I am not going to do some sales thing. This price is not what I had hoped for.

Transition

Do not dwell long in the acknowledgement step. It is meant as a quick, respectful moment, not the time to open a long conversation. We need to follow the steps. After the acknowledgement, move quickly through a transition, to get you to the story. The acknowledgement and transition are necessary to complete the process but move on.

Seller Offer

A transition might be:

I represent you and will always do as you wish. **However, I think it is my job to say something here. Is that OK?**

OR...

I understand that we might want to counter offer and because I represent you I will do whatever you choose. But it is my job to pause a moment.

OR...

I need to be careful here. I represent you and need to make sure that I am not too emotionally attached to the situation. I think it is important that I visit about something with you.

Story

Every year I have a few clients that miss out on what ended up being the best situation on their home because that offer came too early during that "**just listed frenzy.**" Though they all end up selling, they do not necessarily net more.

Or...

Every year I have a few clients that end up going through hell before they get an acceptable offer. I never quite know why but often they had an offer early on that we rejected and then we sat awhile. I am not pretending that I know that will happen to you but I have learned to be careful. It is not fun when we miss our buyer.

OR...

Every year I have clients lose out on what ends up the best or very close to best offer they receive because they counter and the buyer won't budge. We go on and on and **end up with basically the same** offer or less because we get shopped. The other buyers wonder why no one else wanted your home. **This offer does help us to get to** (your dream, they will thank you if you remind them of what is important. Their dream is important) so we need to pause for just a second before we counter.

OR...

If the Market is hot

I have to tell you, it is hard for many buyers right now. In the past, buyers had an expectation of somewhat steady increases in the value of their home, their single biggest investment. Now, after this period of skyrocketing prices, many buyers are getting nervous. We all know this can not continue forever. They are all wondering if that is coming up and if they are the next round of fools, that bought at the top of the market, that everyone will talk about.

Seller Offer 40

I don't know any real buyers in this market that think they can steal something. They just don't want to lose everything when prices adjust.

I think this buyer is probably just trying to buy your home but is one of those that are getting nervous about where the market heads. Buyers don't just accept all counter offers anymore. They did a year ago but prices are getting higher now.

I believe one of the reasons you hired me is because of my professionalism (or honesty or negotiation skills). So, **I am not doing my job if I don't say something.** This offer is not what we hoped for but it does accomplish for us, your number one goal of (talk about their dream) so I am supposed to get us to pause and make sure we give this is good consideration before we make any changes (or raise their price).

OR...

If the market is slow

I have to tell you, it is hard for many buyers right now. In the past, we all had great expectations of huge appreciation with our homes so that was part of the expectation. In today's world most buyers do not assume that their home value will sky rocket any time soon, they are much more cautious and know that inflation will not take care of their dumb move if they pay top dollar. They know they **don't need to steal** a home but they need to be wise **and nobody wants to pay top dollar.** I think this buyer is probably just trying to buy your home but is one of those that are nervous about where the market heads. Buyers don't just accept all counter offers anymore. They are very nervous of where the market is head.

I believe one of the reasons you hired me is because of my professionalism (or honesty or negotiation skills). So, **I am not doing my job if I don't say something.** This offer is not what we hoped for but it does accomplish for us your number one goal of (their dream) so I am supposed to get us to pause and make sure we give this is good consideration before we make any changes (or raise their price).

Close

I think it is my job here to point out that we know the buyer will pay this amount. **Beyond that, I have no clue.** I am not pushing to have you accept any one offer over another but if you could still get to (your dream) with this offer. I think we are supposed to take a close look at it.

OR...

This offer does help us to get to (your dream) so we need to pause for just a second before we counter.

Or...

A young couple have agreed to buy your home. I'm not going to pretend that it is the perfect offer you'd hoped for but it does get us to (your dream) so we should take a serious look at it.

OR...

Seller Offer

After years (or if you are newer, after talking to the best agents) I found that homes almost always sell for market value. There is always a bit of a disparity between the guy that got the most and the guy that got the least.

With this offer we aren't that one guy that got the highest but we are not anywhere near the lowest. This is a solid offer and might be fair for both parties.

OR...

I think you hired me because I am supposed to speak up right now.... or .... **My job is to pause here** and let you know that from my experience, your buyer is probably a human. (pause) **Those darn humans are sooo unpredictable.** (pause) I can't pretend I know how they will respond but I do know they would love your home at this price and that some buyers will walk for a nickel. All buyers are continuing to check the internet while we are talking. I'd like us to consider the price again before we move on. Is that OK?

OR...

One of the things that we are supposed to do, is ask ourselves what happens if we accept this offer and also **what happens if we don't**. Can we explore those separately before we write the counter?

Seller Scripts
Price Reduction

We have all taken an overpriced listing or two. There is great pressure to do so. Some of our competitors purposely lie, as a way to buy a listing through hopes of a stupid high price. Our sellers can be emotionally charged and believe they should get extra for the rock garden their kids built when they were 3 and 5.

Interesting to me, in the old days we would present our CMA and the sellers would be surprised how high the value was. They really had no access to comps. Now, everyone has access to many sources of information. Some of it is even correct. They all know the minimum value and of course, theirs is better than those others.

As a result we still do and always will, have the need to feel comfortable in dealing with price again later.

I love the concept of "The Market Speaks." I let people know that I will do my best and I want to get the most possible, but sometimes I am off by a bit. When I am, "The Market Speaks" to us pretty quickly. We need to listen.

Each market is different as we roller coaster our way through a career. Ups and downs. But in each season there is a norm that sellers should expect if they are going to be one of the listings that sells. Describe to them upfront what that expectation is.

As an example, in a "normal" market I might let them know that we should expect a couple showings right away from active lookers and then dripping 1-3 per week. If we go a month without an offer, we are too high. The market would have spoken. Or if we get 8 showings and no offer, and I check with the other Realtors and those were real buyers, we are too high. The market has spoken.

Price Reduction

Or in a faster paced market I might say, " If we don't gat a few showings the first week and no offer in two weeks, we are too high. We will know that because the market told us. If we don't have a good offer in a couple weeks, we will need to take a look. The market would have spoken to us. If we get 8 showings and no offers and I call the agents and we were not number one or number two on their buyer's list, we are too high."

And this scenario, mostly because someone needs to document this for posterity's sake.... I am in a market where if we do not get an offer in 3 days, the market has spoken. Imagine, if we hit the market Friday and do not sell in two days, I ask for a price reduction on Monday because we are obviously, an overpriced dog.

I want sellers to know that I am willing to try their higher price (only because I couldn't convince them otherwise) and we will market as hard as we can. That will give us enough exposure for us to hear what the market says. If they aren't talking to us, then we should make a small adjustment. Not too big at a time because I really want to get you guys as much as possible. But we should look at it in 3 days or two weeks or... and then see what the market says from there.

If at two weeks, we have had a couple people come back for a second showing or we were close to the top of their list, we might choose to sit tight a bit longer. If we are not near the top of anyone's list, we need to listen and make a small adjustment. We never out wait it because we would look shop worn.

Buyers have enough information to see that you were not just on the market a long time. They can see that you started too high and have been taking small adjustments. If you are now where they need you to be, they will come look.

I do not believe the old shop worn rules apply. It hurts if you sit on the market forever like an idiot. If it takes you a while to methodically find the correct price for a buyer, you are wise. Buyers will still offer when you get there. The key is to keep your client moving downward. If they are too high continually adjust. Do not just sit there.

Some of the Monster real estate agents get their sellers to sign a series of price reductions at the time they take the listing. They get their client to internalize the concept of listening to the market and adjusting accordingly. They get an agreement that gives the exact dates and exact price, when the reduction will occur. Of course, they call their client and remind them the new price is going in tomorrow but there is seldom any discussion. Sometimes we override the decrease if we have a hot prospect looking or coming back.

Here are some sample conversations outside of the "Market Has Spoken" concept.

After years (or if you are newer, after talking to the best agents) I found that homes almost always sell for market value. If we price ourselves too high, we eliminate from the search the vast majority of people that want to buy a home. Most buyers do not try and become a professional negotiator. They will drive by but won't ask their agent to show them the home if we are higher than others they can look at. Most buyers look until they find a good home and then buy it. They might try and be a dash cute and offer something a bit less but most people will walk away from one they like, if it is too high. Most **people don't like offering low**. It makes them uncomfortable. They keep looking.

OR...

I need to talk to you about something. **I believe I have made a mistake.** Remember when I listed the home I told you I thought it was worth $300,000 but after you reminded me of the slab granite and the nice yard I was swayed and thought maybe we could get more. Even though I have done this a long time,

Price Reduction

sometimes I make an emotional decision, especially when I like the people that I am working with. I think I let my emotions get the best of me, but I do care about you guys so now I am here with the tough conversation of letting you know that I think we are priced too high.

OR...

I need to talk to you about something. I know that **I need to have the conversation with you soon about adjusting our price** to make sure we are competitive (or to make sure we don't sit on the market and get shop worn). I have been dragging my feet because I know how much you'd like to get a buyer that would pay our asking price. (or, I like you guys so much and I know you don't want to hear this)

I am calling you today because tomorrow is the cutoff for the magazine ads that I want to put you in. The problem is the shelf life of that magazine is 30-90 days and I don't want to be in there incorrectly. Tom and Sue, since I think we are going to need to make a price adjustment, I recommend that we do it now so that we look good when this ad hits all the grocery stores.

OR...

I believe one of the reasons you hired me is because of my professionalism (or honesty or negotiation skills). So, **I am not doing my job if I don't say something.**

I don't like this part of my job but it is what you are paying for. I have followed up with the agents that showed your home. Most of them have good buyers that have or will make, offers but not on ours. We know we have a great property but it sounds like we were just outside of what they thought the correct value was.

I don't think I am doing my job if I don't advise you that we would be wise to take a look at price.

Seller Scripts
Reduce your Fee

Understand that society has programmed us to ask for a lower commission. They have all heard the ad on the morning commute radio with the agent that has a listing fee of minus 1%. They know you are too high before you mention what your fee is. They have also seen some reality TV shows about flipping so…..

Most people that do ask for a fee reduction, are uncomfortable in doing so. They feel they have to ask but their heart is not in to it. They aren't natural negotiators and have not done much of it before.

Give them the gift of allowing them to say they tried. They now can tell their friends that they went through tough negotiations but chose the best agent over the cheapest.

Don't just cave in. Many sellers have no intention of really negotiating but felt they were supposed to ask. Get that. Do not cave on the first mention of lowering your fee. Commit to yourself that in life, you **never say yes on the first request to lower your standard of living.** Make them work a bit for it unless you feel that really is their number hot one button… which it seldom is.

internalize that the best response when they ask about lowering the fee is…….. nothing. It is important to understand that most people do not want to have this conversation and are uncomfortable with this part.

GO SLOW. Don't just spit out the perfect response. **Pause** like you are surprised or you need to let that sink in before you respond to them. Talk slowly and thoughtfully. Pause before you answer throughout the whole discussion on fee, to drag it on a bit.

Reduce Your Fee   48

Conversations are similar to:

"No." Say it with a bit of a chuckle and move on. This is not for every situation but I have used it when it worked and we never brought up fee again and I have surprised some with my flippancy. It is sort of fun to do because it allows you to be "caught off guard" by the question a bit. You say the no with a bit of a startled chuckle or surprise at the question.

OR...

I understand why you would ask. I have found that there is s huge disparity amongst agents. In our community 10% of us do 90% of the real estate transactions. Can you imagine that? There are a ton of agents that list a home and hope we will sell it for them. Those of us in the top 10% really earn our fee and are committed to giving great value for the dollar. I have clients tell me that my **negotiation skills alone are worth the entire fee**. I am committed to help you **net** the highest amount possible when we get to the closing table and to look out for your interests. Wouldn't you rather have that than a discount broker with no experience or marketing or negotiation skills?

OR...

(if this is true for you.. or use days on market... or...)

I understand why commission is a big part of this. It affects your net dollars when we are all said and done. Let me show you something interesting. Look at this, in our MLS the average agent **sells his listing for X% of the original list price**. If you look at this column you see that my sold to list price ratio is 4% (the real number for you) better. That means that because of my marketing and negotiation skills, my clients average a 4%

higher gross, which after they pay all the fees, nets them 2.5% more. I have learned over the years that **all Realtors are not alike and what I do has real and measurable value for my clients**.

OR...

I actually have a commission reduction program but technically you don't qualify yet. I charge a lower fee for my clients that give me referrals to their friends. I will reduce my fee by X% (or dollars) if you introduce me to someone that decides to do business with me before we get to closing. I usually reduce my fee by X% if I am working with a client that has sent me multiple introductions to potential new clients.

OR...

Actually Tom and Susan, I usually charge 6%, but I give a 1% discount to my repeat clients. I should have mentioned that earlier.

OR...

If at anytime during the listing agreement, I am not performing to the highest standards that should be expected with a X% fee, you may have the listing back (or reduce my fee then). No questions asked.

OR...

I'll be honest with you, **to an extent all Realtors are alike** in that they put up a sign and throw the home into MLS and they all have a website... and that has a value... not a real big one but something.

Reduce Your Fee

We find that **additional** marketing tools and negotiation skills are needed in order to **increase the odds that my sellers will get top dollar.** They find that their net is higher and the experience goes much smoother if they work with you know, me.

OR...

If the fee wasn't an issue, whom would you hire? Ask them why they would do that. If it is you have them re-iterate why you are better. Then ask them if that has value to them. If yes but not enough, tell them one more thing and ask if that has value.

If it is not you, differentiate yourself and show what you do that has additional value. After you show your additional value, ask, "That has to have some value, right?"

OR...

I believe in my heart that my fee is a good value. I will represent you as if you were my sister. The sister I like. (OOPS... Sorry Mom)

OR...

I made a business decision awhile back. As my business was growing, I had to decide to go for the money or do I commit to providing the best service I could dream up. So I bit the bullet and hired an assistant. (committed to a web designer, stager, photographer) She/he is fabulous. That is expensive but it guarantees that no matter how busy I get, I have the perfect person making sure that my group gives the best help and service to all of my clients. I thought about going the money route because then I could easily reduce my fee a dash when everyone asks but then I couldn't always promise that I will exceed your expectations in my responsiveness and overall results.

I really hope that business model works for you because I believe it nets you more in the end and I love your home. It would be really fun (or an honor) to help you make a move.

OR...

One of the reasons **sellers pay us more than the discounters** is that we use professional quality photos (or free staging or high tech stuff, cool stuff or the team or experience). Today the buyers are all over the internet to search for their home, and statistics show the quality of the photo is the number 1 thing to keep them engaged in your home. I believe we get more showings for our sellers just from that one thing. **More showings, has to have value, doesn't it.** (or whatever you do, your high tech stuff, your team, your marketing , your stager or experience or.... but tell them why you have value and then ask them, **that has to have some value, doesn't it?**... Just one thing... If you don't get a commitment try one more thing and then ask again... "That has to have value, doesn't it?"

OR...

I'd say I have the best money back guarantee. When we get right down to it, you don't have to accept any offer unless you felt I was worth my fee and the complete package is good for you. Is that fair?

OR...

Reduce Your Fee

(be careful with this one but if you do, say it laughingly, literally, laugh while you say it because if not you could be arrogant and annoying, hmmmm..)

"If the house doesn't sell, how much did you save?" ....
(I told you, be careful)

OR...

If you paid a higher fee but netted the same or more, would you work with me?

My last thought is to remind you to make sure that you clarify that "fee" is the only reason, that they have not already signed a listing agreement. We only solve the fee question, if it is the only question left on the table. That is important. Solve everything. When you get agreement that you are the one except for your fee, justify your fee. If you can not justify it, make a decision. Take it and be grateful or move on. If you decide it is a good piece of business ask them:

"If I do...., will you list with me?

Seller Scripts
Friend in the business

Back to that part about there being more licensed real estate agents in the county than there are humans and dogs combined. We are going to have competition from someone that is not as good as us but has the inside track. That is serious competition.

If it comes up don't just ignore it. If it is on their mind, help them to find a reason to tell the friend, no.

Acknowledge to them that you understand that can be hard. Make it easier for them. You might try the following process.

The pause is important. Do not handle this like you have the words all ready to go. Pause and be thoughtful for longer than you want. Let them know that you understand and are giving a thoughtful response. This is not an objection like price. A price objection comes from their logical brain. Not wanting to hurt a friend or Uncle Fred is much different. Have empathy.

Pause
Acknowledge
Story
This is business
Minimize
Move on

Friend in the Business

Try words similar to:

Pause...I understand and believe me almost **everyone I work with has** a relative, or a relative's boyfriend that just got his real estate license or a friend that is a part time Realtor... sometimes seems like half the population has their real estate license. I understand that you don't want to hurt them. I really do get that. Interesting though, locally, 10% off us do 90% of the business. We bump into the same agents over and over. It really is an important transaction for you and you **might consider looking at it like business decision**. It matters whom you list with to maximize your equity.

And the other (laughing) part of it is that really you might be doing your relationship with that person a huge favor by working with an unattached professional. We even joke about it in the industry how we should never work with a relative (or friend) that we like... only the ones we don't like. Buying/moving can be a dash stressful at a couple different times of the process. It is nice to go through that knowing you can let off a little steam on old Bob and you do not have to turn around have **Thanksgiving dinner with** me.

OR...

We even joke about it in the industry how we should never work with a relative that we like... only the ones we don't like.

OR...

I understand that is a sensitive issue and it comes up all the time for me. However, since this serious business and how much you net, makes a difference. May I take a minute and show you why it makes business sense to work with me?

29 Monsters

Look at this, in our MLS the average agent **sells his listing for X% of the original list price**. If you look at this column you see that my sold to list price ratio is 4% (the real number for you) better. That means that because of my marketing and negotiation skills, my clients average a 4% higher gross. I have learned over the years that **all Realtors are not alike and what I do has real and measurable value for my clients**. I know I'm not a cousin but as s business decision I believe I am the best choice. May I go to work for you and show what we do to net you more money?

OR...

I'll be honest with you, **to an extent all Realtors are alike** in that they put up a sign and throw the home into MLS and they all have a website... and that has a value... not a real big one but something. We find that **additional** marketing tools and negotiation skills are needed in order to **increase the odds that my sellers will get top dollar**. They find that their net is higher and the experience goes much smoother if they work with one of the top agents (or a pro)

OR...

If you have developed a niche, you might let the seller know that it will be easy to explain to the licensed relative that you would love to work with them next time but in your **neighborhood, there is a specialist.** She really knows this niche better than anyone.

OR...

(or whatever you do, your high tech stuff, your team, your marketing, your stager or experience or....) but tell them why you have value and then ask them,

"That has to have value, doesn't it?"

Just one thing... Give them one thing you do, that you could tell they appreciated and ask if that has value. Then close them. "Does that make sense?" OK. Thank you.

Then if necessary another reason, one item at a time. Just get to "Yes that has value" and be done. Do not give them 8 reasons together. It is cleaner and an easier process to get a thumbs up or thumbs down, on one item at a time.

Seller Scripts
Random Thoughts

Here are some random thoughts and scripts that I jotted down during my journey. These either didn't fit elsewhere or I was too lazy to mess with it.

How do you feel about what we've talked about so far?

Do you have any suggestions on how you would like to see the home marketed?

Do you have any questions about my marketing plan?

Do you have a target move date in mind?

I'm excited about helping you. Can we get started while I'm here?

Are you OK with open house this weekend?

What would you say are the best features of your home?

Do you have an opinion about the best place for the sign?

Can we get going and get your home on the market now?
 If no, "why not?" Often it is such that you can say " that is a little thing. Let's get going and maybe the buyer won't even ask you to do that."

How do you feel about what we covered so far?

I love your home and I am really excited that I might get to work with you. Do I get to be your agent?

Random thoughts   58

I am really happy because I love your home and you are such a nice person. I feel that you are going to pick me as your agent and if so, that's really exciting for me. I'd be honored to help you.

Sometimes it is a good idea to get the home inspected before the buyer requests it. It does create a fee of about ... that you probably won't normally have, but it let's us deal with any surprises ahead of time and allows us to show the buyers that the home has been inspected and here are the results. Do you have interest in that? Would you like me to set it up with someone I trust?

OK, I gotta tell you. I would love to represent you because that is what I do and how I make my living. But now that I've met you, I know I would really enjoy working with you. I have been so fortunate that most of my clients are really nice people and it makes it so much more enjoyable to help people like you. I really enjoy that process and it's so much better than just getting paid. I hope that is OK to say but I would love to work with you guys.

I start the process with getting my stager (inspector, handyman) out here. I am hoping he can do that tomorrow. Does that work for you? Good. I just need to get your approval to work with me. or.. That way I can start representing you before we actually go live in the multiple. Is that OK?

If at anytime during the listing agreement, I am not performing to the highest standards, you may have the listing back. No questions asked.

In our industry, one of the ways we measure performance is by (expireds, sold/list ratio, days on mkt. etc.) let me show you how I rank compared to the other agents you might interview?

29 Monsters

How soon am I able to show the home?

Am I able to hold open house this weekend?

I am going to need from you, a key to put in the lockbox and then I will do the rest.

Why I might not be the selling agent

After I list your home, I am completely committed to getting it sold. I try very hard to sell it myself which does happen about x% of the time. The industry average is single digits but my number is higher because I really try to show my listings whenever I can.
However my marketing often attracts buyers who already have an agent that they are working with. I want you to know that I will completely support those agents and their buyers in any role I can. I am not a pig and will make sure I chase any potential buyer even if they are working with a different agent. I am known by the other Realtors in town as an agent they can trust, so they often let me do part of their job for them. I am thrilled to do that if it keeps things moving for my sellers.

Purpose of an open house (If you want an open house)

I am not going to pretend that we will get hundreds of potential buyers at the open or that I will write an offer on your home on Sunday. The goal of the open is to **attract attention** to the home. Sometimes that works and sometimes it does not. Many buyers that have an agent will be out looking without their Realtor. I am thrilled to have them come and then leave to talk with their Realtor. At least we got them inside. Yes, I might meet a buyer

Random thoughts

that wants a different home but I will make sure they have seen yours first. The **open is not "the answer" but it is one of the many things we do to make sure we capture all the possible buyers.**

Another agent gave us a higher price

Of course there was. Some companies actually teach that as **a listing strategy** for their agents. They train them to take the listing at a price higher than the other agents will tell the sellers and then they have a long term strategy to hassle you and **work you over to get the price reduced** after they have you under a binding contract.

I just can't work that way. I have to bring honesty and integrity to my business. (Or I've done this too long and need to maintain my reputation, or it would make me hate my job if it was to work you over.) Besides the agents don't decide what a buyer will pay. We can only estimate value by looking at what buyers are paying for similar homes. I am not supposed to just give you a number, so that you list with me.

Wouldn't you rather work with a Realtor that is honest? Eventually, when we get an offer, it will be much easier for you to make the right decisions if you have a professional in your court that you trust.

Higher price gives us room to negotiate

I get that. But it is fascinating. I have spent hours analyzing **the sale price to list price ratio**. There are some exceptions but the vast majority of homes sell at the asking price or very close to it. I think when buyers have choices, they just move onto the next one when they look at an overpriced home. Very few tell me, I'd love that one if it were priced right. They just move on and very often when they find the best house that is priced right, they just buy it before someone else does. By being priced right we might get some low ball guy that we have to reject but most likely we will attract an offer from someone that is serious about buying a home **but isn't a professional negotiator**. Most buyers **are just humans that want to buy a home** for their family. I think that is whom we should market to, don't you?

Another quick buyer script

Now you need to know that though I work very hard for clients, I am not a super salesman. Often I think I know when we are in the right house that you should buy. Problem is, sometimes I am wrong. If I know it is the one I just ask people if they want to try and buy this one. If I am not sure I am not going to do some sales thing and try and ask you to start buying every house.

So here's the deal. When you are in a home that you like a lot, you have to tell me. It doesn't mean you are ready to write an offer but it helps me. Tell me if a home is close or maybe even the one. O.K.?

Does that apply here?

Referral scripts

Throughout the transaction we usually get positive feedback from our clients via email, on the phone or in person. When they tell us why they are happy, remember it and write it down. When the time comes to ask for a referral, repeat back to them their words. As an example, maybe they stated how appreciative of your help they were and it meant a lot to have an agent they could "trust." Not then, but at any later meeting you can say "Would you trust me to help your friends when their time comes to move?" If yes, Who do you think will be the soonest?

OR...

I am really glad about the price we got on this property. Now I hope you know that when you introduce me to people you know that need my help, that I will be just as diligent in getting them a good deal too. Are you comfortable doing that for me with your friends?
Thank you. If you were a betting man, who do you think will be soonest?

OR...

If they expressed appreciation that you were so available, later say "It has really been nice to work with you. I just want you to know that if you give me an opportunity to work with one of your friends that I promise to be available for them whenever they need me.

OR...

If they have said I am nice we go with nice. If they said I am professional then I commit to being professional for their referrals. Whenever possible we use the same words that our client would use in that sentence. We keep them in their Happy Place by using words that are in their normal vocabulary. And if we are lucky enough that tell us what they like about us…. Commit to being that person for all their referrals.

The best way to get a referral is to provide great service and deserve the right to receive one. If you are uncomfortable getting around to the conversation, use a transition script. That is a separate chapter.

Once you get there try any of these scripts. I suggest that you pick 3 or 4 and practice them. Have a few different scripts that flow off your tongue when you need them.

Help

Understand that people like to **"help"** other people that they like, if it isn't a big inconvenience. Try:

I'm really trying to grow my business. May I ask your advice on something?

May I ask you a business question?

May I ask for your help on something?

With any of these types of questions, ask permission as above first. Then tell them what you need. Are you trying to identify a particular type of prospect or hoping to develop a certain niche? Find something that they will be able to do. Ask them for referrals to people they know that are moving.

A Happy Current Client

Can I tell you something I have learned? When I have a client that is great to work with and are good people, like you guys, well those people when they give me a referral, have friends that I also love to work with. Go figure, eh? Nice people know nice people...

Sooo, I have to tell you if you guys are the type that are willing to speak up when you bump into somebody that is thinking of moving, and introduce me to them, I would really appreciate it. I bet I would love helping anyone you sent me.

Let them speak then ask "who came to mind when I said that?"

At the Beginning

My goal is to make you so over the top pleased with my help, that, before we are through working together, you introduce me to someone you know that could use my help. Matter of fact, I will probably ask you that a couple times along the way. Is that OK? Thank you.

OK here's a practice run, when I said that did anyone come to mind?

OR...

May I tell you something about my business model?

My objective is to focus on the client that needs my help right now. Most Realtors, spend the majority of their time chasing potential new buyers and sellers. I am able to do that only because my clients and friends introduce me to people they know that need my help with a move.

I bring it up now because almost everyone gets so excited about their move that they bump into a couple other people that are thinking about moving as well. When that happens would you be willing to give them my name?

Thank you so much. When it comes up, please call me as well so I know the call from your friend is coming.

We do that for two reasons. First: It scares off some referrers if they think the process is to have them call us back with a phone number so that we can call and harass their friends.

This keeps them in their comfort zone. They just gave your name and it is very non-threatening to their friend. They just called you to give a heads up. Then when they do call and tell us about the referral, we ask for the friends name and number. It is much easier for them to do so after they told us they referred us.

It is not enough to give your name out. You need to be able to call them. Teaching our clients to call us with a heads up allows them to relax about telling their friend and then we get the information we need, on that heads-up call.

If no one comes to mind

Thanks anyway. I appreciate it. It is uncanny how often, just because we talked about it, you will think of somebody in the next couple days. Will you keep me in mind if that happens?... or
… May I call you Monday and see if anyone came to mind?

3 Clients

Let me ask you something, I have found I have 3 types of clients,
1. Folks that run into situations all the time where people are moving and introduce me to them.
2. People that once in awhile bump into somebody that could use my help and is glad to share my name.
3. Some that will never refer me or anybody ever.

Which of those are you, can I ask?

OR…

It is often suggested that if the person you ask does not have anybody come to mind, that you probe areas of their life to trigger a thought. Such as " how about anybody from the kids soccer? How about at church? " and so forth. I get it. If it works for you, stay with it. However, be careful because it can be annoying. I recommend that you narrow it to one or two suggestions if at all. You do not always use the same triggers. Fit them to the person. If they are young look for 1st time buyers. If they are wealthy look for investors.

If they say you are Great:

(DO NOT say "no big deal")

My pleasure. That was a tough one. You have been a joy to work with and I am excited that we are on the right track to ...(name their dream).......

May I ask you a favor? I have found that the people I enjoy working with the most, you know the nice people like you, have friends that are probably nice people. I love my job when I can help a friend's friend with their move and try to exceed their expectations. It makes you look good and I love it and I get to work with nice people. There must be someone in your circle that is considering a move sometime. Who, of your acquaintances is probably next to move?

They say they referred me:

Thank you so much. That means a lot to me. May I make a request? I have found that in todays world and the nature of the internet that people get side tracked so easily and next thing you know are connected with an agent that you wouldn't exactly have recommended. Just someone with a good web presence or bought their info from Zillow or somebody.

Would you object to me calling them as well?

Referral Scripts

OR...

Thank you so much. Here is what I have found, telling her is the easy part. The hard part is making sure we really connect up to have a meaningful conversation in person. Do you have any ideas about how I best accomplish that?

OR...

If they say they tell people about you all the time

Fabulous. Thank you. Which of them do you think will need me the soonest?

Who, of all your acquaintances, is the most likely to move next?

Phone call to database for referrals

Hi Tom, how are you? Good. There are 2 reasons I'm calling today. I wanted to talk to you about…. And then I have a quick business question for you.

Sooo, how is ….

Tom the second reason for my call is, I am refining my business model a bit. My focus will be on helping my past clients, friends and their referrals to me, almost exclusively. That way I am able to give much better service to the people I care about than when I am out trying to chase around meeting new buyers and sellers. I was hoping you might be able to help me out.

OR...

Who, of all your acquaintances, is the most likely to move next?

OR...

If you were me, what would you do to continue to develop towards that goal of working exclusively for my people and their friends?

OR...

The market is really active right now and I want to make sure people don't miss it. Is there one of your friends that I should visit with about what's going on?

OR...

If you do run across someone, please don't keep me a secret.

OR...

OK, (or thank you). Now, next time you are at Bingo (church, kids soccer) and someone mentions just maybe sorta kinda possibly moving, don't keep me a secret.

Referral Scripts

Out of area referrals

Ask your wealthier clients if they are thinking of buying a 2nd home. Let them know you have a pretty good referral network and will check out that area for them.

Scripts
Referral Transitions

I talk separately about the words to use when we ask for a referral. For many that is the easy part. The hard part is getting there. We struggle getting from talking about the grandkids soccer game to "Do you know anybody who is thinking of moving?" It is too great of a leap and we struggle.

I worked for a large franchise for awhile and they taught us the old "Oh by the way….." at the end of a conversation. It always sounded phony to me. As if I didn't call to ask for a referral and then just happened to think of it as I was hanging up. Surprise. Seems dishonest and phony. Use it if you like. Many do. Not me.

Let me suggest that you develop transition scripts that set up your referral request script. You need to have a path from the grandkids to business that flows for you and the client. Here are two ways to do that:

First: Find opportunities to talk about the real estate market. For starters, people are always asking us about the market or how is business. I suggest you never again answer that question with something like "Great.: What a waste of an opportunity.

If someone does not ask you about how the market is, start the conversation with: Can I tell you what's going on in the real estate market? They always say yes because everyone is vested in the real estate values personally. Then we can tell them our story.

Decide ahead of time what type of client you are most likely to get a referral to, from this person. Is it most likely a first time buyer, an established seller, an investor etc. Build a story around each one of those scenarios and be prepared to tell it.

Referral Transitions

The story should be real and interesting and lead them to who would be the perfect referral for us to receive.

If we just ask for a referral, people usually can't think of one right off. When we tell a story that describes someone that is benefitting from my services, it helps them think of someone in a similar position.

As an example: if the inventory is low your story might be:

"It is fascinating what is going on right now. The poor sellers that got hammered a few years ago are really in the cat bird seat. Quite a few of those folks that wanted to move a few years ago waited because of the low prices. Now those that did, look like geniuses. It is really fun right now to help some of those folks that are downsizing. It is a really good time for them to get top dollar."

Then shut up. Do not go straight to "Who do you know?" The goal is to get them **to visit about real estate** for awhile. Let them talk and see if they acknowledge that or agree with you or… Create a conversation that they engage in about real estate. Try and go back and forth awhile like a real conversation between two people should be.

Then: You can get to, "When I talked about that, did anybody come to mind that might also consider if moving now makes sense?"

OR…

"It is very interesting. After the banking crisis, financing really tightened up. It was necessary but a killer for the first time buyer. I can't believe it. Things are loosening up again for those first timers. They still need to have a job but the millennials can get a home now finally, if they want one."

OR...

"Wow, this is historic stuff and very fun to be a part of. There is a huge backlog of demand in our area and we are predicted to have 10% population growth over the next decade. I am not a fortune teller so I never know for sure where prices go. One thing I can tell you is there is huge upward pressure on rents right now and for years to come. The guys that are buying rentals right now are cutting a fat one.

Another great way to keep your transitions comfortable is to tell them upfront that you are going to ask them for a referral or at least talk about business. That is way better than pretending that you just thought of it. On a phone call try:

"Hi John, this is Bob Bloom. How are you? Great. Say I have been wanting to call and visit with you guys and then before I go I also wanted to talk about business for just a moment. Then proceed to normal conversation.

OR...

Hi Jane…….. I have 2 purposes to my call, to catch up with you and to ask you a business question. Is that all right?

You need to write and practice transition scripts that make it comfortable to bring up the subject of getting a referral or asking about their plans.

Affirmations on Steroids

I would like to explore the value of doing daily affirmations as well as some hints as to how to make them be effective. They can be meaningless and a waste of time or turn you into a Monster. The good kind of monster.

It is very fun for me to introduce you to positive affirmations because I bet none of you have ever heard of them before, right?

OK, so maybe you have. You have probably even tried them before and either ended with "What's the big deal" or they were helpful but you eventually got away from them. If you are like me, you saw some positive effect and then just eventually spaced out and didn't do them anymore.

Two things happened to me that got me to a place where I finally got it and committed to doing affirmations. Doing them the correct way.

First, I had read Gary Keller's The Millionaire Real Estate Agent before and liked it. There was a lot of information there and I somehow skipped right past the part about affirmations. When I re-read the book a few years later, it sunk into me what he had said. This was not some self-proclaimed guru saying to do this. Keller had interviewed dozens of the top agents in the country to see how they built and ran their businesses. These guys all did numbers like a hundred million in volume. You know, the freaks of our industry.

Every one of them to this day, still does positive daily affirmations. I stopped and had to re-read that part again. These guys have already made it big time. These were not new agents or failing agents that needed an emotional bump. These were the pros and that is what they all believed was an integral part of their continued success. All of them.

29 Monsters

One of the points of the book was that we are supposed to model successful people and do what they do instead of re-invent the wheel. Hmmmmmm, they all do daily positive affirmations. Hmmmmm, I wonder if I am supposed to learn anything from that statement?

Second, as part of a commitment I made to myself, I read a hundred books in a year. Books that might be helpful to me in my personal and business growth. By doing that, I read some incredible material. I, for the first time, read about research that had been done by clinical psychologists. They analyzed the behavior and the brain wave activity of people that were doing affirmations. They also tested people that were at different stages of habit change sand consciously improving their willpower.

For me to get excited about something enough that I am going to add or change a habit, I need to see some scientific evidence that backs up the theory. I am not suggesting you be that way, it is just how my brain works. If I see the empirical data it is easier for me to believe it is true and thus buy in. Now I had Gary Keller's anecdotal evidence and scientific proof to back it up. My little pea brain says, "Let's go."

I am not going to walk you through the statistics and study results. Keller says they all did affirmations. Science confirms it. And in my sample, 25 out of 29 Monster Real Estate Agents did them. Funny part to me, the 4 that did not, are so positive and confident that they don't realize they are a walking positive affirmation. If you want to do your own research, cool. Me I am going to start at the assumption that your life would be better over time, if you chose to do positive affirmations and do them correctly. Let's also assume that they will not have a huge impact on your life if it is something you try for awhile. The biggest and best, incorporate them into their life.

So here we go:

Affirmations

First you need to choose what areas of your life you would like to focus on. They should touch all areas of your life including, spiritual, personal relationships, career, fun and giving back to society.

In order to get the most out of them, they need to be tied to a passion and emotion. What is your BIG Why or your divine purpose? That thing that would be off the charts cool, if you could achieve. Identify the good habits or character traits that you either have and are proud of or would like to develop further.

Write them down but they can't be about money or I want to build a big real estate career or I am going to sell ten million in real estate this year.

The words would be more like:

"I am a monster Realtor because I give such incredible service and great value to my clients."

"I am a creative person that shares my thoughts and ideas freely with no expectations in return."

"I am constantly giving out love to all people around me and am continually grateful for all of the love that is returned to me."

" I have a huge business and a fabulous personal life because I have a positive impact on the lives of the people I touch."

" I have a positive impact on thousands of people's lives."

" I am at the perfect stage in life to build a huge business."

" I am known as an upbeat person that gets results."

" I am kind of a health nut and look and feel great."

" I make a ton of money because I deserve it and give more than I receive."

"I am a great parent and am making wonderful contributions to my family."

"I am a kick ass guy that has a fun life."

29 Monsters

" I am thankful for the perfect past I have had that got me to this exact point in life. It has prepared me to now go be the best that I can be."

"I am at the perfect stage in life to build a large real estate business. I have much to contribute to others."

"Because I find the good in all people and always show kindness to everybody, it is fun for me to meet new people and potential clients."

" Everyday, in every way, I am experiencing personal growth."

" I am constantly growing in my spirituality and am an example for non-believers."

" I am known as an upbeat guy with creative ideas."

" I am a good catch for my spouse and I am very appreciative to have him/her. I continually do the little things that let her know that I love her."

" I am grateful for the place I am in my life and that I have the health required to go be whomever I choose to become."

You may notice that they are all focused on the positive and there are none that read like "I will stop being a bum." We do not try and change a habit by focusing on the habit. The focus is on the replacement activity or lifestyle or mental shift.

There are some learned men like Dr. Wayne Dyer, who believe that your affirmations and goals need to be aligned with a God-like purpose in order for them to come to pass. If we want something and it does the world a benefit, we are more likely to get it. Focus the affirmation on your intent to do good and create or add value for others, in order to achieve success.

Visualize the Process

Research shows that subjects that visualize the process needed to go through on the way to their goal instead of just the goal, had quicker results. As an example have some of your affirmations be similar to these:

"One of the reasons that I always have such a big pending volume is because I know it begins with lead generation which I am consistently good at."

OR...

"I have come to enjoy cold calling. It is fun for me every time I succeed to know I am getting closer to my goal."

OR...

"The more often I go to the gym the easier it becomes. I like seeing the results. I am really proud of myself for adding a resistance program to my workouts. I don't say it to others but I am really looking goooood."

Second. Write them down. Duh, right?

Third, we do not read them twice a day. That does nothing. The brain is wired to passion and emotional things and doesn't give as much weight to things of logic. We do not read in a monotone voice " I am a great Realtor that gives great value to my clients." We add passion and emotion. We close our eyes, we read them aloud, and then we wing it. We change the words around as we think about it. More like " I am a great Realtor that gives great value to my clients. They love me and I am always very busy.

That is fun for me because I really like people and get a total buzz out of helping so many different folks. It feels great to be one of the best agents in the county and it is so nice that my clients think of me as a real pro and the best agent they have ever worked with. I like being so well respected and though I am humble, it is pretty cool that I have achieved this status as one of the go to agents."

OK, you get that? Take your affirmation and read it and then close your eyes and expand on it but more importantly really imagine how it feels to be one of the most respected agents around and how proud that makes you feel. Hear the words of thank you. Feel a hug from a happy client.

Without spending too much time on this part, researchers have measured brain waves when their subjects were on a roller coaster. They measured them when participants read an affirmation about liking roller coasters. They also measured them when people tried to really feel the affirmation of being on a roller coaster.

Guess what? The brain waves were exactly the same when they thought about it with emotion as when they were actually on the roller coaster. Exactly the same. The brain waves were almost flat lined when they read the sentence about liking roller coasters. We need to add emotion and really feel what it would be like. Notice the word feel. Imagine the feeling of being loved or respected, or excited or traveling because you are so successful etc.

Fourth, add extra dimension to your affirmation such as color, sound music and touch. Imagine that you can hear the carnival music that is playing when you ride the roller coaster. What color is it and what color shirt are you wearing. Really feel your loved ones hand that you are holding while you ride it with her. Feel the goose bumps on your neck and the wind in your face and imagine that you are throwing your hands in the air. It is the same for all of them. Put a face to some people that are thanking you for being such a fabulous Realtor and really feel how proud you are. Smell the cookies that they made for you as a thank you treat. See the green trees in the background of your favorite restaurant that you took them to when they gave you a referral. Smell, touch and see the situation with great joy and emotion. Great joy. Really. Feel it.

Fifth: We have all heard that it takes 21 days to create a new habit right? And we have all heard that it takes 30 days to create a habit, right? Well both of those things are nonsense. They are just some well meaning self help guru saying something clever. Really by saying that, it has done you and I a great disservice. We believed them and tried very hard to change a habit for 21-30 days. When some magic didn't overtake us we quit and said "That affirmation thing is stupid."

The scientists looked at the topic through accepted research methodology. They have found that it takes between 5 and 300 days and everybody is different. However, most of us cluster around 50-100 days. Not 21.

Be patient and take a long-term approach. Assume when you start that it is proven to work and all the big agents do it. Assume you will do it for life. You aren't specifically looking for results. You are just committed to follow this new way. Somewhere along that path, it will become instinctual. It will probably be so gradual that you won't notice when. It doesn't really matter because you knew this was the new you from the beginning. Then some-where around 2-3 or 8 months you will find something starting to change. Who cares when that happens because you already committed to the change and not to just try it for 30 days.

Sixth: The time needed for positive results and the degree of success, were helped exponentially by the test subjects including **meditation** into their regimen. Preferably, you sit down and add great emotion to your affirmations and then meditate for a few minutes. I'm not going to bore you with the science behind it. I'm just telling you that has been tested and effective.

Personally I love meditating. There is a lot of data available to help teach you how at the library and on the internet. I highly encourage you to check it out for 2-3 months. Don't stop too soon because you will continue to get better, with time.

Seventh: Make sure you include some affirmations about **what you are grateful for**. It trains your brain to identify the positive and thus shorten your affirmation success cycle. Be appreciative for your unique talents that you are developing. Be thankful for your perfect past of good and bad. The series of life events that have made you who you are now. The fabulous you that could only get here, by traveling that path.

Eighth: Give your self some rewards along the way. Not a specific every week kind of thing but set a time frame that if you stay at it you will reward yourself. Vary how long that time frame is.

Lastly, your affirmations are not set in stone. As you progress, change them up from time to time. Let them evolve as you grow. Add and subtract from them.
You will also find that as you let your thoughts wander around each one, the words will change. Adjust with those changes. They are a direction not a specific end point.

I know it is not a new topic but hopefully I gave you a different slant on it. I hope that you succeed with them this time. I didn't get it the first 48 times someone tried to teach me about them. Maybe the reason that you too have heard from all the book writers about this concept, is because the successful people all employ this habit. Hmmmm....

Affirmations for Referrals

Remember that affirmations to be effective, must be from the heart. They have no value if we are a bad person and are saying positive affirmations. The brain knows you are lying. Affirmations are worthless if they come from a place of greed. Our affirmations are based around who we are at our core. Who are we when we are at our best? What are our strengths that we need to develop and focus on?

Here is the process:

1-- Identify who you are at your core. What are strengths? What are you best at? Why should people work with you? Are you honest? Do you answer your phone, unlike most agents? Are you hard working, have a sense of humor, great at marketing or technology? Do you create a stress free transaction for your clients?

2-- Internalize that many agents do not deliver a fabulous experience. That is part of this. Acknowledge that there are a lot of real estate agents that aren't that great. The client's friend will move whether or not the two of you ever meet. The only question is whether or not you deserve to work with that person? Statistically speaking, are you a much better choice than what might happen, if you don't speak up. It usually requires you speaking up to create the opportunity to do good. By doing good, you receive.

3--- Understand that you are doing your client and the referral a favor by doing your job and asking. If you are good and many agents aren't, you are doing them a huge favor by saving them from those lousy Realtors.

29 Monsters 83

Some examples might be:

I have reached a place in my career where I realize that I really am one of the best agents in the county. I give superior service to my clients and treat them with dignity, honesty and respect. Because I am a professional, I have internalized that "only by giving do I receive." I always put my client's interests first. I would rather not get paid than harm another. People in the community have come to know that I am honest and fair. They know I represent my clients well.

My clients enjoy doing their friends the favor of introducing me to them. They know that I will treat them great and that the alternative for their friend, is some random agent. That is scary.

Because I deliver a better moving experience for my clients, their friends are lucky when I am introduced to them. I completely understand that I have an obligation to my community to build a larger business. Because I am so unique in what I bring to their transaction, it is my duty to represent as many people as possible. I can only do that if I ask people that like and trust me, to help me accomplish that.

. It is right for me to ask for referrals. If I don't, their friends, statistically speaking, have a pretty good chance of having a bad real estate agent experience. It is not Ok for me to hear about it later and have it be too late for me to be able to help.

As one of the more honest, hard working and compassionate agents, I owe it to my clients to make sure people they care about, do not have a miserable moving experience. That is a big part of my job, to ask people for referrals.

(If you are religious add what you feel) I am grateful that God has given me such talents. I know that God loves everyone as much as me and gave us each unique gifts. He did that because we are all needed to make the world it's best. People are supposed to use their talents to make a great contribution. The

Referral Affirmations 84

baker, cobbler, artist, fireman, teacher and preacher have all found their God given gift and are using it to it's fullest, to make the world a better place. I appreciate their contribution... their gifts are different than mine and I am glad they have them. Thank you to them for their contribution. I am glad they used their gifts for all of our benefit.

If I am to be complete and live in the likeness of my Creator, I am supposed to excel at what I do. I have been given many gifts that really make me special and able to help people that are moving. This is not a sales thing. God has given me many attributes that I need to use. (Now think about which those are for you... Perhaps, have empathy, care about people, not shy, hard worker, reliable, responsible, able to think on your feet, good listener, persuasive, honest, able to reduce stress for clients, creative.....) Whatever your gifts are, be appreciative and commit to using them.

If you are a believer, the key is to commit to using those gifts now, for the honor and glory of your Creator.

Affirmations for Closing

Closing is not a trick. It is not some cute thing we do to make a bunch of commissions. It is nearly impossible to get someone to the closing table on a home that they don't like but were "sold." Closing is not trickery to benefit us. It is the opposite. We close because it is in our clients' best interest.

Here is the process:

1-- Remind yourself that you promised your client that you would help them.

2-- Acknowledge that moving is very stressful for many people and that makes it hard for them to make a timely decision. It is huge decision and people get frozen in fear. Many people have never bought anything close to this expensive and it is scary.

3-- Our job is to get them into the best home possible. If we are so mellow that they miss the home they want, we should have our real estate license taken away. If we said we would help and we do not help them by closing them, it is unfair on your part.

4-- It is very cruel, unethical and a very weak behavior on your part, if you won't do your job. Help them.

Because of all this, it is really comfortable for you to speak up and try and take control when it is needed. Here are some affirmations that might help keep you in the right frame of mind:

I committed to help my clients. That was not lip service but something that I believe in my heart. I have an obligation and responsibility to help these human beings when the time is right. I

Closing Affirmations 86

will not let them down by not trying more than once to help them trough the stress of a normal closing process. Because I am a professional, I know how important it is to the people I committed to help, for me to do my job. I am strong enough to not let them miss the opportunity, because of me. When it is my turn to do my job, I will not be uncomfortable speaking up and leading them. They hired me to do this and I would let them down if I gave up too easily when they need me most.

I have reached a place in my career where I realize that I really am one of the best agents in the county. I give superior service to my clients and treat them with dignity, honesty and respect. Because I am not only professional but because by internalizing that "only by giving do I receive", my clients are appreciative that I am willing to speak up when they need me the most.

Because I deliver a better moving experience for my clients, I realize I have an obligation to all of the sellers I visit with about real estate, to close them. I need to close while I am still in front of them. Statistically, many will get tricked into working with the wrong agent after I leave. I owe it to them to try more than once to help them avoid that possibility. Because I am in the business, I understand that risk better than they. I have worked with agents that were not very good and I know some I wouldn't choose to work with if I were a seller. I am an insider and have that information. The sellers do not. I have an obligation to get the paperwork done, at the soonest opportunity.

It is my job. My clients are appreciative at the end of our transactions when I was willing to do my job and help them through a stressful decision making time. I committed to these human beings that I would help them, so I will be strong enough to speak up when it is my turn. I committed to do that. That is my job. All of my clients are thrilled if they can get to closing on the home of their choice. I need to make sure that I help them do that.

29 Monsters

As an insider I understand much more than my clients, the need for urgency. If it is the right home, we always move quickly.

It is my job and my moral obligation to close when the situation is in my client's best interest. It would be wrong of me to just run around and let people in houses. I understand anyone can do that. A robot could do that.

The reason I feel comfortable telling people I will help them is because I will. When I know it is the right house, I will not let them lose out on it. I guess I am a bit competitive that way. I want my people to win the house hunt game. We will be quicker to see the best ones and first to offer. That only happens if I close them. They need me to do that.

2nd Best Database

We are continually needing to build and nurture our database. I have nurtured people for years and they absolutely loved me. They looked forward to my calls and would use me as their local real estate expert if they had any questions or were curious about a property. I slept well at night knowing that I had a database full of clients and future clients that guaranteed my future pay checks.

I love meandering through my database and looking at all of my future pieces of business. However, no matter how much love these folks give me, every year I get a few annual occasions when my clients excitedly tell me how they moved and I would be so happy for them. They thank me again for all my help and they never could have gotten house #2 without all my help on house #1. They hug me with glee as they tell me how they didn't like their recent real estate agent near as much as me but aren't I happy for them?

No matter what we do, we will lose some of our database folks to another agent. I assume you have realized that real estate agents are a dime a dozen. They may not be very good but there are a lot of them. It is hard for people to say no to the new son-in-law, the golf buddy or your neighbor when it comes to pick a real estate agent to represent them. Their neighbor, friend or cousin will know that they are thinking of moving way before you will. Their mom probably will pressure them to use Uncle Ernie over you. Sorry but Ernie goes to Thanksgiving dinner every year.

No matter what we do we always have competition that we don't know exists.

One of the best database segments that you can develop is the out of area owners. They are the most loyal. They are loyal because their golf buddy and neighbor may be real estate agents but not in your market. They are loyal because they don't receive several subdivision Realtor marketing pieces and they do not hear the 1% commission radio ads for your market. When you have developed a communication with out of area owners they call you when they decide to sell. Who else would they call?

We have had recent past markets where people with money did not necessarily sell their home when they moved. Many kept the old home so they could buy the new one at a low price but not get killed on the low value of the one they were selling. Because of that there are still a lot of owners that probably would choose to not be a landlord. Their time might be now.

Beyond that, there are always absentee owners. People inherit property. People move away with the intention of coming back and never do. There are investors that came in to your market to buy but do not have a local agent that they know and have a relationship with.

They are easy to find with the help of your title company.
Here is the 7-step plan I would follow.

#1   I would establish an identity complete with business cards and letterhead that states you are the "out of area" real estate expert. It would be different than your local branding that you use and only seen by the out-of-towners.

#2   Drive by the property and take a picture. Make notes of the condition and of the best amenities.

#3   Send them an introductory letter with a picture of the home. Emphasize a picture of any area that the tenants are not caring for. The seller would want to see that.

#4   Phone them. Yes you are OK to do so. Make it as a follow-up to ask them if they would like you to swing by a couple

2nd Best Database

times a year and send you an updated photo of the condition of the property.

#5 Google them to find interests that might appear. Build a database just as if they were local and find reasons to call them.

#6 On future calls make a point of exploring one new area to find their interests. One time ask why they moved there. Once ask what they like most about there or miss from here. Etc. Treat them like any database client. Mail them your newsletter and call them once or twice a year.

#7 Every year or so mail them a photo of their home. If you notice it has spring flowers planted, go take the picture in the spring. Same with fall colors, after a huge snowstorm or when the lawn looks great or terrible.

This has to be the most loyal group of potential clients you could ever develop. You will be seen as their connection to their real estate back home. Very little effort and no competition.

Boomshackalacka....

Great Referral Sources

The goal for many of us is to reach a place where most of our business comes from past clients and referrals. We nurture our past clients forever. All of them.

However, we need to identify and then treat differently, the people that are likely referrers. In our database we segment out the referrers into their own group and give them special attention. Some of those likely referrers are past clients and some are not. Here are a couple thoughts about targeting referrers:

First: Every professional that is in **your INNER CIRCLE** of your real estate business must reciprocate or they are out. Simple as that and no exceptions.

They will squawk and say we don't understand. Your inspector, lender, handyman and escrow officer will say that they don't meet people until they already have an agent and bought a house. They'd like to help but I am apparently too simple to understand how real estate works. They wish they could support my business but… blah, blah, blah.

Every person in my inner circle is a human. Every human has neighbors, kids in school, outside interests and/ or family members and friends. Why would the people who I give business to, be any different? They can give us referrals if it is important to them. Perhaps through their work situation or perhaps from their other circles. We train our clients to give us referrals and I will not let the people that I give business to, be any different.

Tell them that you love them and hope to never switch but it has been brought to your attention that a lot of people want your business. They seem to be willing to give me referrals in return. Let them know your expectations are low but zero doesn't work.

Great Referral Sources

Give them a few months and then call back and remind them, if you have gotten nothing.

If it doesn't happen, I bet you will find that there really isn't just one good inspector, lender, handyman, painter, escrow officer etc. in your community. Do not give me the garbage that you tell your clients. Do not tell me that you have the best escrow closing agent and .... Whatever.... Nonsense poopy pants. There are other great ones in every community.

Ask around and interview a few. Pick one and support them as long as they do their job and support you.

Second: Analyze your database and identify who are the people with large spheres of friends and acquaintances. Some people are involved in everything from volunteering, to having the teens at their house, very active socially or been in the community forever and just plain **KNOWS AND SEES LOTS OF PEOPLE** on a regular basis.

If you have a client that loves you and is committed to give you every referral they hear of but live a happy, unassuming and fairly private life... well. You will get her nephew when he grows up and buys a home in 11 years.

Identify and then focus on developing the people you have met that are the type that are always interacting with a large group of people. Spoil them. The broader their circle of influence, the greater your chances of finding someone that will give you lots of leads, not one occasionally. More is better in the referral world.

Third: Identify who would be able to give you a **STEADY STREAM** of clients and target them with a long-range program until you get them. Build a program that does not take lots of your time. Commit to consistently focusing on this great long-term strategy. Target groups like estate attorneys, bankruptcy attorneys, divorce attorneys, financial planners/ estate planners, accountants and wedding planners. It can take awhile to get these people but very few agents target them with a long range effort. Once you have their business, you will have it forever.

In this same category, it is a fabulous idea to slowly earn the trust to be the residential referral source for the local commercial real estate agents. They really don't want to be bothered with this and aren't really the best agent for their client's residential needs. Nice steady source of upper end clients.

Fourth: Give to get. Go through your database and identify whom you might be able to give referrals to. People want to support the people that support them. Which two of your database folks could you connect together or just plain give a referral or somehow add value to them or their business.

It is fun to think like an extension of their company and try and find them a piece of business or a nice business connection.

Fifth: Do not make the mistake of thinking you ask for a referral at closing. You might ask then but what you really do is ask early and/or when they are happiest.

I know you all have happy clients at the end. I get that but sometimes after we dealt with the many issues and small decisions and meeting deadlines, some people are a bit worn out by the process. Explain to them at the beginning that most of your business comes from referrals and that if they know anyone who is just thinking about it, it means a lot to you.... If we have a happy event in the process, often that is a better time than waiting until closing to talk about it. Plus if you wait until closing you don't have as much contact with them and they easily can forget to call you to give it to you. **ASK EARLY & OFTEN.**

If you get a referral to a client, tell them on the first appointment that you work by referral. They are not unusual. The majority of your clients come from your other clients. Tell them that it is the same with them and you will be asking them if they can think of anyone whom might be moving, from time to time.

Great Referral Sources

When they agree that is OK, immediately say "Let's practice. While I was saying all that did anyone come to mind that might be able to use my services?"

Last: you need to have a specific searchable segment in your database to track everyone who has ever given you a referral. **Referrers refer.** If they did it once and all parties were happy, they will do it again. It is important to thank them appropriately and continually show the respect they deserve. They will refer again if you keep in touch and make them feel appreciated.

New Words=New Results

I propose, that the words we use, matter. It makes a huge difference in our results, because our clients react differently, to different words. Different words=different results, sometimes.

Many buying decisions are made from the heart. Often times, they are made from our emotional world. Some of you say I am wrong, because it is all price and fee. Sometimes that is true, but even then, you are more likely to get an opportunity if the seller is "Comfortable" with you. Maybe not consciously, but we all would rather work with folks we are comfortable with, than those we are not.

Words are part of our memory bank and their impact won't be forgotten. We associate certain memories and feelings, with certain words. If someone uses words that have a negative connotation to you, you are uncomfortable. If they use the words that have pleasant memories and associations, then you are more comfortable.

The words that I use are comfortable to me. The same is true for your clients. Use their words. Listen, and when appropriate, use the word that they would have used, in that sentence. We need to be aware to speak in words, that are in our client's normal vocabulary and thus, in their "Comfort Zone." Those are the words that will make them feel warm and cozy and very comfortable.

Many of us "introduce" people, from time to time and are comfortable with the process, concept and the words. We are not as comfortable "referring" someone, and have never been called upon to give one before. The last time they received a referral, they ended up half-naked in a cold room, with a proctologist.

People have warm feelings around the words "friends" and "family." If it fits your personality, refer to your client base as your

New Words=New Results   96

"family of clients." Use the concept of, a closeness and a sharing, between all of you. Make a point of saying, "Welcome to the family" and hold reunions. When you introduce them to each other do so as, cousin Fred and Aunt Betty and make it fun. If you can't go that far, understand that those words, are better than client or customer, from the warm & fuzzy perspective.

People don't want to be "satisfied" with your service, they want to be "happy." Satisfaction either sounds like part of an overused, meaningless, guarantee or a Rolling Stones song, and we're not going there. People want to be happy.

If they say they are going to the beach this week-end, don't later acknowledge you love the shore. You love the beach.

If they show you their yard, do not love the lawn. Love the yard.

If they say "How bout them Dawgs" don't next time say, "Man, the Huskies are doing great." The "Dawgs" are doing great.

Maybe they have a spouse, but it might be their honey. Some people have a dog and some a puppy, pooch or best friend. Some folks have time to grab lunch but others would rather just grab a bite or get out of the office. I know people that exercise and some that work-out, while even others go to the gym.

Don't over do it. Do not sound like you are mimicking them, because they will pick up on it. It is better to use their words a couple minutes after they did, than a couple seconds later. If it is an uncomfortable word for you, either don't use it or acknowledge out loud to the person "That is a funny word I never really use… Hmmm,(then repeat it) that's a pretty good word for that use, "Do not let them think you are being cute so go slow but just remember what word they would have used, in that sentence.

Most people like to "help" someone, if they can and if it is not a huge effort for them. Ask people to help. Tell them you are focusing on growing your business and you were wondering if they could "help" you out, with something? "Help" is a comfortable word for most.

29 Monsters

We don't use the words "reticular activator" because those are our words, not the average person's, when we are asking for a referral. They are more likely to use the word "subconscious", which they are familiar with and a word, they have used before.

This is a great example of my point. We ask people for their business or for a referral, when they are in a "happy" place. If we use words like "reticular activator" to describe the process, their brain says "Say what? I don't know that word. Time for class, while Bobbo teaches me about that. Better get out of this emotional, I love Bob, happy place... and go to my logical side."

Then we ask them for….. OOPS…. That might have been a good time to use their comfort words and just get 'er done. We can be cool and impress people with our big words, another time.

Try to be a pro without sounding like a walking dictionary. Keep your words in the listener's language and comfort zone.

To Phone or Not To Phone

To phone or not to phone, that is the question.
Whether tis nobler of the mind to suffer
the slings and arrows of outrageous prospects
or choose to drown in a sea of busywork.

To phone or not to phone, that is the question.
Perhaps, we phone no more and die a salesman's death.
To nap. To sleep perhaps to dream, but there's the rub.
For in that nap of death, the dreams may come.
Oh to stop, the dreams of success unachieved.
The nightmares of a wasted life persist.

To phone or not to phone, that is the question.
Destined to grunt and sweat under a weary life
where fear has made a coward of your soul
or take a stand against mediocrity?
Perhaps do the thing that's hard, almost too much
and thus by so doing, achieve your best.

To phone or not to phone, that is the question.
A silly man sits by the phone and waits
perchance to hit the phone-in lottery.
While a simple man picks it up and dials.
To dial. To dream of calls answered with glee.
Prospects waiting for someone to call, Alas

To phone or not to phone, that is the question.
     Duh, dial it.

Quitters Prosper

(No matter what your mama told you)

This is a fabulous concept. I hope you love it, as much as I did, when I first learned of it.

I liked the idea of it, before I even read about it. I saw a title, "Zero Based Thinking" and I knew immediately, this book's for me. I'm not the best at math, but any formula built around zero…. I can keep up with this one. In grade school, the "zero question", was always the trick question. I am ready, for any zero based multiplication, addition or subtraction they throw at me. A little fuzzy on how to divide by zero, but 3 out of 4, I'm liking the odds.

The theory behind "Zero Based Thinking," is that you need to ask yourself, in many different areas of your life,

"Knowing what I know today,

would I make that same decision, today?"

Some say it a little differently and ask,

"If I was an outsider, looking at this decision, and I now have all the information that you have gathered over time by living this situation, would I choose to get involved today? Would I handle this the same today?"

Quitters Prosper

You know where I am headed. **Sometimes quitters prosper.** We are supposed to stand back and look at the decisions that we have made, and put each one of them on trial. That individual, stand-alone decision, knowing everything that I now know, would I choose that again? Would I choose it now, if I was not currently, already, involved in it? Was it a good idea or a bad idea?

We should analyze our career choices first. Since we are real estate agents, we start there. Is this the right field for you? Do you fully appreciate its advantages enough to offset the disadvantages? Do you feel passionate about either growing or doing this well?

If you do not have excitement for this work, you must leave. It is a really hard job to do if you don't like it. Find what you are passionate about and pursue that. Set up a step by step process as to how you get to there from here.

Was real estate a great decision, in hindsight?

Is it a great decision, moving forward?

Mama used to say "You can't look in hindsight." Nonsense. You not only can, but you must. Of course you can't change the past, but just because you made a hasty decision once, does not mean you have to live with it, forever. Once you figure out that it was not the best choice, change.

You still have a lot of life left, so move-on and make a good decision, now. Bad decisions can be offset, by good decisions.

29 Monsters

Next, look at the way you go to market. If you were starting fresh today, would you develop a certain niche. Would you create a monster database to work from? Would you sell commercial or specialize in downtown properties.

If you were being taught by the best in our business, would you approach things differently, this time? Would you commit to learning scripts? Would you focus on a higher price range?

Now that I know this business...

How would I coach someone else to do it

Take a look at your business with fresh eyes. Your fresh eyes. If you were an outsider looking in at how you go to market, what advice would you give to you?

It is **not just the things we chose to do**, that were our decisions. We all also know the things that we passed up, didn't have the drive to go after, or just ignored as an opportunity.

Those too were decisions, and should be put under the microscope.

Knowing what I now know, should I do it today?

If you are very brave, ask this same question of how you spend your spare time. Knowing what you now know, would you really have spent so many nights in front of the T.V. or down at the bar or cheating on your spouse? Too late to take those back, but with the new approach to decision making, you affirm the path forward, as a new conscious choice. If you now know you shouldn't be doing something, stop. Make a different decision this time.

Quitters prosper

This same analysis should be used with our clients. Aye Yi Yi. Some of these folks drive us crazy.

In 1978 I was a young Realtor and hungry. I would work with anybody and I hoped, everybody. I met an investor, let's just call him Paul, whom bought a couple houses with me, sold one and listed a several hundred thousand dollar mobile home park with me. Understand, that the year before, my 1st year in the business, I did 2.5 million in volume and my average house sale that year was $32,000. In my market, it would take me 23 more average-priced home sales, to equal this one mobile home park commission.

Booyah....

I know what you are thinking. You think, I figured out to go into commercial real estate and lived happily ever after. But noooo,

I had my annual board meeting, by myself, at the beach and voted to fire him. It was fabulous. It was the highlight of my year. This guy drove me crazy. He was a whiner and was never happy, never said thanks and depressed me…. Well, not clinically depressed. However, I would start my day excited and ready to kick butt and after one phone call with, the one we shall call Paul, I had to get out of there. I would end up going for a drive, wondering what those college kids were picking in that cow pasture. They seemed to be a lot mellower than I was feeling. (It was the 70's after all, so no judging)

I called, the one we shall call Paul, and told him I didn't think we were a great fit and it would be in his best interest, to find an agent that would make him happier. If it were today I would have said….

"The one that we shall call Paul, You're Fired."

29 Monsters

Do not be Rodney Dangerfield. Have a little respect. Really. If you have a client, that uses you as a whipping boy, don't do that. When we get abused and beat up, we get tired. If we choose to deal with some nightmare customer, it destroys our career and marriage.

That is a little dramatic and yet not. The energy sucker client has a lasting effect. You don't get off the phone and say, "I feel great now." No, it leaves you depleted and having less focus and energy, to tackle your real opportunities. It is a huge drain on your other activities. It leads to lower production, going back to flipping burgers and your spouse saying he/she never wants to have sex with you again.

As a real estate agent coach, I hear, "I have so much time invested into this client, that I can't stop now." You know, in for a penny in for a pound. Whoa dare, Pardner. Duh, just because you wasted a lot of time, does not make it a good idea to, statistically speaking, waste a bunch more time.

Cut Your Losses

If you are a real estate agent and not yet in escrow, do not pretend that you must be getting close and about to get paid on this one.

If old Bob, knew everything you know about your business, would I choose your business or business model today or a different approach?"

We always hear about that inspiring success story of the guy who made it. That guy. He failed a dozen times along the way, but now he hit the big time. It is often told as a story of persistence. They even made up a saying that, persistence pays.

Well, maybe that too sometimes, but often the guy was not persistent at all. He was just a quitter. (as his mother-in-law says "Can't hold a job".... not that, that applies nor do I have lasting nightmares) No, the guy was not just another stinking quitter, he

Quitters prosper

was a Quitter, with a capitol **Q**. He quit more stuff, than most people start. The kids on the playground would have chanted, "Quitter, Quitter, Quitter," but instead he is hailed as a Hero of Persistence.

As these successful people travelled down their career path, they would continually stop and put their past and current decisions, on trial. If they now have enough information to know it was a bad decision, they made a change. The world saw them as failing, over and over, until they found the right niche and then they were instantly persistent, in seeking success. In reality they were practicing ZBT, Zero Based Thinking and when the answer was obvious, they bailed. Not persistent guys, just bailers.

Put your career decision on trial. (I know a great guy, that had a fabulous and rapidly climbing career at Kodak, who you older folks will remember sold a thing called film. We took photographs with it… and mailed it off for developing) This guy quit and became a Realtor.

Put your work habits, business model and career direction on trial. Be the business coach that will be honest with you. You probably already know that you should make some changes. With what you now know, do you need a different approach to this career?

Analyze your marketing, database development and especially your niche or lack of one. If you started today would you focus more? Would you have consistent brand building marketing to your chosen clients?

One of the greatest obstacles to change is the resistance to change. Duh, but really. We get in a comfort zone. We settle, because it is uncomfortable to do
otherwise. We need to internalize, that we should at least make the analysis. Would I choose this, right now, if I was an outsider considering my choices.

If it is no, realize, that comfortable feeling, is the #1 factor in making a decision. You just decided it was a bad decision. Are you really going to continue to make a bad decision, after you have identified it, as bad? Some will say yes, but I hope ever so slightly fewer of you, after having read this.

Today is the zero point, in Zero Based Thinking. Everything starts over from today, ground zero. You just have better data to make your decision now, than when you first made it.

Need a do-over? Call it.

The Price is Right...

Mrs. Neighbor….. Come on Down….
You are the next contestant on…..
The Price is Right….

We all need to continually add people to our database. Doesn't matter how large yours is, we all lose some of them. We will not do business with them all and some drift away and use…. our competitor…. Uncle Ernie.

I am assuming you have built your touch systems. Any new additions to your CRM just flow and maintenance requires little effort. The problem is finding ways to attract new legitimate folks that agree to let you keep in touch. They must agree to let you keep in touch to be of any real value.

It is easier to gather those new prospects when we have a purpose to do so. Most of us are not going to go cold door knocking. If we did, our results would be minimal. Without a purpose to knock on the door, it is shut quickly. If we hold open house all we gather is a bunch of emails that eventually block us.

Here is one idea to solve that. This can be done with every listing you ever get, 80% of the listings that your entire company lists and any home that you hold open house in. Hmmmm, that's a pretty good start.

Hold a "Guess the Sale Price" Contest

We are all aware that we should door knock around new listings. That really is effective as a way to build a database. Most of us don't do it because that activity produces limited results in getting a neighbor to list with us now. That is how it was sold to

29 Monsters

most agents. "When a new listing goes up, a bunch of neighbors will want to sell too." My experience says, not so much. Occasionally but if that is the goal there are better activities.

It is an easy way to get neighbors to see you as the local pro and agree to receive your marketing. The goal is to identify neighborhoods that you would salivate having any listing in. We then follow our company listings that come up in those neighborhoods. None of the agents in your office will be door knocking their listings and all but a few jerks would be happy to let you do so. Do not pretend that it is your listing. Let them know that your company has a new listing.

Combine the purposeful excuse of the new listing with a fun "Guess the Sales Price" contest and many people will stop and engage with you. If they are willing to play along and give you a price guess, you will have multiple reasons to have a light hearted and non-threatening follow-up communication with your new prospects. You can mail them a thank you. You can follow up when it goes pending. You can build suspense and not tell them who is ahead until closing. Maybe you can make a chart and show the prices that were guessed so they see where they lie. Maybe you take out seller concessions or maybe not.

This game creates a CMA conversation, without having to have one. You can engage multiple times with someone who has the perfect comp, in their neighbor. They will be interested and when it is all over, you have established yourself as a friendly professional that works their neighborhood.

Do the same at open houses. Have all that come through, enter the contest. They can not enter with just an email address. You need their info. It gives you a chance to gather more names and numbers than is normally possible. You have a light-hearted reason to follow-up and an opportunity to try and represent these buyers. Much easier conversation than haggling over getting their phone number.

The Price is Right 108

It doesn't take much of a prize. I got local restaurants to give me free dinner certificates. Most of them actually have an allowance to give them to the community for different events and reasons. Let them know you will promote them to the neighbors and all that see the home.

You might consider running a small portion of your next ad, that states, "Play Guess the Sales Price" on the following listings......

Maybe your gift certificate retailer could co-sponsor and get their name out there. Maybe it could be a fun thing that people in your community start to associate with you. They will see your ads to play. If they are in your chosen neighborhoods, they will get an invitation to play. When they see your company sign go up, they wait for your door knock. They might win one. They might never win and you can tease them as the unluckiest client you have. Maybe it would be a fun connection that sets you apart and attracts new people that would like to be in your database. I love "Bob, May I please also receive your mail?"

Farming

Most of you have heard of the idea of farming an area before. That has been around forever but is often not successful for most agents. I believe it is a fabulous idea if done right, not the way us old timers did it.

First, the old concept of farming a subdivision is out. Just not enough volume in any one subdivision no matter how big it is. You will never get ever listing in any farm so the area has to be bigger. Here's what you look for:

An area that is identifiable. That would be a section of your town that people call something and identify with. In my county it might be Felida, Salmon Creek, Mt. Vista, Fisher's Landing etc. These are not subdivisions but areas of town that hold between 4,000 and 10,000 people. The area needs to be big enough that it has at least 4,000 people but not so big (10,000 is pushing it), that you obviously do not dominate it. The people in that area have to consider that is where they live and preferably are proud of it. You can make a terrific living if you get a high % of the business in an area of 7,500 people.

Next it has to be an area that you would enjoy working and be proud to say that you are the King or Queen of.

Pick a price range of homes where you can make some money because once established you will spend a lot of time there, your whole career. I would not suggest a starter home price range. It is no more effort to make a medium sized or big commission as a small one.

Go into your multiple and really analyze turnover in a few areas. Most communities have a huge disparity in turnover, if you really look. There are some fabulous parts of town I would love to work in but nobody moves.

Farming 110

I have access to the county records and would go from one home to another and see how long they have lived there. You could also figure the population of an identifiable multiple listing area and then compare the # of solds to total folks. Maybe look at an area where executives move in and out because of its proximity to the airport. Look at a few pockets of homes and compare.

When you identify a high turnover, upper end area, check you multiple to make sure there is not one dominant agent there, first. It is rare but check.

Now, build a brand. You need an identity that clearly states that you are committed to that area. It needs to be your brand and logo and slogan and all over your letterhead and business cards. Make sure a seller can say, "Wow this is an agent we should interview because they obviously specialize in my neighborhood. I suggest brands like:

"Queen of Felida"
"King of Salmon Creek"
"Fisher's Landing Specialist"
"The Ridgefield Neighbor Pro"
"Condo King"
"Alameda Expert."

Something that states right out of the gate, that you are their local area specialist.

Be aware that **you will need two sets** of business cards and letterhead etc. When you are in your farm you use one set and when you get a referral to someone that is not in that area, you use your regular company card and identity.

Then act as if you own it. Go door knock every "just listed" and "just sold" home as if it were your listing. Don't lie about it,

29 Monsters

but set up a query and be the first to preview each new listing. Make a flyer that you door knock with about that home before the sign is up. Let people know that it isn't your listing but you are the local specialist and wanted them to know about it.

When a home closes that you weren't involved in, wait a week and then go meet the new owner and welcome them to the neighborhood. Let them know that they are in your area now and you will keep them updated as to what is going on. Put them in your database. By the time they go to move they will think you sold them the home.

As your data grows, stop and call a neighbor that you have met, before you call on a FSBO or before you go on an appointment. Tell them that you are going to go see the guy down the street and ask if they have they met them. Ask if you can use their name.

That does two things: it gives you a chance to call your database with purpose and show that them you are still active in their neighborhood. If they do say to use their name, it changes the whole mood of your appointment. You have turned it from a cold meeting to almost one from a referral.

Make sure your open house signs have your brand on it and use lots of them. Lots of them…. so everyone sees there is the King again.

Learn everything about the area, from who homesteaded and other history, your favorite restaurants, info abut the schools and sports teams, average income and other demographic info, the politicians etc. etc. To be the local specialist make sure you know more than the people that live there, about their area.

Identify which people in your database live there. When you send out your monthly mailer, make it different than the rest of your mailings. Make sure it is relevant to them or at least uses your specialist brand identity. That means that you need a database system that allows you to set up your own searchable queries. I currently recommend realtyjuggler.com. (No, I do not get paid)

Farming

Develop marketing pieces and your 8x8s that include some that are the history of the area or fun things to do in the area or anything very specific to them.

Be the expert before you door knock. If someone asks you about a property that is listed or just sold and you have to answer that you will check and get back to them, you are definitely NOT the local expert.

That means you need to preview the listings in that area. If there are a lot, I would start with those that have been listed a longtime. If you preview a home and leave your card that states you are the area King, when the owner gets home and sees your brand they are going to wish they listed with you. They will be saying my worthless Realtor didn't even show our home and this lady is our specialist, the Queen of... here..

You will need to follow the expireds. You can say, "I remember your home and I loved the... whatever...and they will be thinking, "hey this is that specialist I wished I had used." That is very powerful. You have seen the home, been identified as the obvious choice and then call them when they expire. Let them know that you don't really work expireds, like all the other 200 calls they will get today. You specialize in their area and noticed they came off the market. You love their home and remember it well. That is why you are calling. You are the obvious choice, not one of the possible choices.

Personally, I would not send out direct mail to the whole neighborhood. It would be a good idea but is pretty expensive and if your advertising budget is big enough, do it. Rather, I would find a pocket here and a pocket there where you had a piece of business and met the neighbors or where you door knocked for the "just solds." Develop pockets that you put in your database and then nurture them with great urgency.

29 Monsters

You don't need to work FSBO's. Just work every FSBO in your farm. It is a completely different call. Introducing yourself to someone if you are the expert that knows everything about their area, is different than I specialize in harassing FSBO's. Let them know that every buyer that wants their neighborhood, eventually finds you.

One of the nice benefits is that you stop losing business to Aunt Judy's boyfriend that is a part time Realtor. It is much easier for the owner that has to see this guy at Thanksgiving, to be able to tell him, I would have used you except we have a local specialist. I will use you next time for sure.

In your marketing pieces, make a joke out of who would you rather work with an agent who focuses on selling acreage and downtown condos and the east side and the historic area and of course your area too, now that they have a GPS and can find you. Let them know that who they work with matters and they should work with the industry's, only specialist in their area. People get it.

As a Nebraska boy I am tempted to talk about rotating your crops and ditch irrigation and the challenges of organic farming but I will save that for another day.

This is a fabulous idea. You can choose the market that most of your business comes from and instead of being one of many agents interviewed, you will be the one that they call when they are thinking of selling. The commercial real estate brokers have done this for years, maybe we should learn from them and be willing to make the big money.

Farming

- Find an open and hold it open as often as possible. Always door knock around it.
- Use lots of signs and have a recognizable logo.
- Door knock around everybody's new, pending & sold
- Meet the new when they move in.
- Go to garage sales
- All FSBO & Expired in area
- Call DB folks about the FSBO 1st
- Area specific newsletter
- Area specific marketing pieces (only specialist, #1 in area)
- Develop pockets within the area
- mini CMAs before door knock
- Meet Employers
- Take pic @ diff. seasons of homes and area landmarks
- Local Convenience Mart on your team
- Develop touches around the area
    - Trivia
    - History
    - Road etc. name history
    - Politicians, famous people
    - Demographics
    - School activities

The Bond Market

I talk about a concept of being the smartest person in the room. It is important to be able to speak intelligently about whichever segment of real estate that your client feels they are pretty educated in. Realtors get tricked all the time into looking clueless… because they are… about the bond market. I know agents that responded with a "Whoopie" when a client told them the bond prices were crashing. No……. there is an inverse relationship. Lower bond prices means higher interest rates and vice versa.

What is a Bond?

A bond is a loan. Bonds have a predetermined interest rate and maturity date that never changes. The bond issuers have credit ratings just like we have credit scores. Their rating affects the interest rate they will pay on their bond. Bonds are usually sold in $1,000 increments, which we call their face value or par value.

Bonds are much safer than the stock market. You will not have the ecstatic rides up that the fabled stock investor will get in "Bull Markets." You also will also not experience the depressive downside of a "Bear Market." No huge gain and no huge loss.

How do they work?

Bonds are considered "fixed income" investments because you know ahead of time how much you will receive and when. Those do not change with the market conditions.

Mortgage bonds offer the investor a great deal of protection. The principal is secured by a valuable asset that could

The Bond Market   116

theoretically be sold off to cover the debt. However, because of this inherent safety, the average mortgage bond tends to yield a lower rate of return than traditional corporate bonds that are backed only by some corporation's promise and ability to pay. This safety is what keeps mortgage interest rates low. Backed by houses.

Conditions that tend to push interest rates low are:

-- **The stock market doing poorly (bonds safer)**
-- **Political unrest internationally (provides a safe haven)**
-- **Slow economy (few investment choices)**

     Investors that are nervous, love to put some of their money in the bond market. If they are nervous that a war in another part of the world may erupt, they want to hedge against the market unease that comes with that and move to the bond market. That keeps interest rates low.
     If investors are scared that the stock market is due to go down, they bail and protect their principal by putting in the bond market.

Conditions that push interest rates up are:

-- **A bull stock market (because fewer bond buyers)**
-- **An expectation of good times and peace ahead**
-- **Trying to slow a too-fast economy (avoid inflation)**

     The fewer buyers there are, the higher yield those buyers get. The old, supply and demand deal. If most investors are out chasing higher returns with their money because they expect growth ahead, then the few left bidding for these bonds, won't have to bid quite so high.

29 Monsters

Because the interest payments you receive and the payback amount and time are fixed, the only thing that can change is the value or price.

If the rates of return available in the current market place go up compared to your old bond, then investors will pay you less for your lower fixed rate. If interest rates go up, the price of your pre-existing bond go down. If interest rates go down then the current value of your pre-existing bond goes up.

How does your fixed rate, compare to what the currently available other options, for investors are?

There is an inverse relationship between price and interest rates.

The interest rate for homeowners is always higher than the bond rate to have room for the banks, investors and mortgage brokers to have a fee.

Bonds are issued by large corporations that need, to raise money. They might be cities, counties, the federal government and in our case, Fannie Mae, Freddie Mac, Fha and other secondary issuers of mortgage backed bonds.

The price of those bonds changes throughout the day just like the stock market is constantly changing throughout the day.

Expireds for Wimps

It would be hard for you to deny that most expired listings are homeowners that want to move. Our job is to find people that want to move.

Most of us hate "working expireds." The routine of calling them at 7:00 A.M. to be first or be respectful and be the 51st agent to offer their services, is draining. Most expired sellers stop answering their phone by about 9:00 on their expired day.

You know with every call that you really could help these folks. Yet they will feel so badgered on expiration day that you don't have the heart to pile on with your clever banter.

I have found that one of the most annoying aspects of the expiration game, is that the real estate agents all say how great they are and how active they are in this exact demographic as the seller's home. Really? If you are the greatest Realtor in my neighborhood, why didn't you ever show my home. It was on the market for 90 days. Where were you then?

I have to tell you, that is a valid point. We all pretend that we could have sold it and we have a ton of buyers for their home but…. Where were you for the last 90 days, if you are so hot? You never once showed my home.

Fair enough. If you hate working expireds and all the sellers hate us working expireds, don't work expireds. Work "expired homes that you showed." What a difference for both you and the seller. You won't have all the hang-ups of forcing yourself to be the harasser of innocent expireds. You will only call people that you have earned the right to call. The seller will be thrilled to hear from an agent that knows their home and tried to sell it for them.

29 Monsters

That phone call goes something like this:

"Hi Mrs. Seller, this is Bob Bloom from XYZ Realty. I know you are getting hammered with a million phone calls from all of the Realtors that works expired listings everyday. I promise you that is not me. But I did have to call you. I love your home. I remember the master bedroom has a view of the valley and I love your kitchen. I was only able to show it to that one couple but I love your home and have been aware to try and show it again if I could. Then I saw this morning that you just expired. I have to tell you if you are still thinking of selling, I would be honored to visit with you. I just love your house and would try really hard to sell it for you.

Do you think that feels any different to the seller? All morning they have heard the egomaniacs tell them how they could solve all their real estate problems, easily. Trust me...

You call and tell them the specific features of their home that you loved and why some buyer, will also love their home.

Let's be honest. This is only for the people that know they should work expired listings but don't and won't because they hate it. There will be way fewer listings to chase if you rule out all the homes you did not show. It also assumes that you are active in a particular area or price range enough that you really have shown the occasional home that ends up expiring.

However, for a fairly active agent to be able to add a dash of expired listing chasing without going into depression, this is an answer.

Expireds for Wimps. Only work the expired listings that you have shown. The call is very relaxed and comfortable to make. Your odds of winning are greatly improved.

Fastest Niche Development

I loved this idea when I heard of it. This is one I never did but would have loved it when I was building up my database.

If you follow this plan, in one year you will have a large database filled with homeowners that see you as an expert in their area. In the area, that you have chosen.

First: choose an area and price range that you would love to see yourself as the dominant player in. Pick a niche that you will love and that is very profitable. It needs to be in the average price range or higher.

What is the ideal group of people that you would like to see yourself working with for the next 20 years? If you could be the Queen of 5 subdivisions, which 5 would they be?

If you picked an area, here we go.

We have all heard about the right things to do when we get a listing. There are 4 contacts that can easily be made with the neighbors of that listing.

The Four opportunities are:

Just Listed
Open House
Pending
Closed

Imagine a new agent that might get 12 new listings their first year. Oh my gosh... at the end of one year you might add 48 people to your database with this program. YAWN...............

Do you think a guy like old B-o-b cares about 48 people. DOUBLE YAWN.

29 Monsters   121

Noooooooo, take that idea and put it on steroids. Do every listing in your company…. No, better yet, every new listing that any agent in town gets, if it is in your chosen areas that you are the King or Queen of. Do them all. At the end of one year you should have a few hundred people that live in your favorite areas that see you as that area's expert. Boomshackalcka, baby…

After one year you can be done with the building phase for your entire career. Head to "nurture" the heck out of them. They are your chosen clients for the future. Of course, continue to market around the new listings in your areas to be a monster, but you won't need to.

In a very short time you could have a monster database that gives you more business than you can service. Just treat the other agent's listings' in your area, like they were yours. If you are the Realtor that wants to be the go to agent in an area, treat every piece of real estate activity as if it is interesting to the neighbors and you are the area specialist. Door knock around every listing in your area when it lists, goes pending and when it closes. Every listing from every agent that is in your area.

Understand that almost no agents do what we all know we are supposed to do. Don't worry about running into the listing agent out doing what you are doing, around his/her listings. They are not there. If they are, almost always he or she will just send a postcard. You will have already met the neighbors before they get the card and you will be seen as the local expert. Plus I think I heard somewhere that we are in a relationship business. People work with agents they know like and trust. Be the first to get to know them.

I am NOT talking about doing anything illegal or unethical. We obviously tell people that it is not our listing. We are just the neighborhood expert. Don't ask a mamby pamby in your office, if they think it is a good idea. It is. Just be honest and only share information that is available to everyone in the world on the internet.

Fastest Niche Development

So, you say you hate door knocking. Me too. It is very hard to knock on a long procession of doors with no purpose and ask if they are thinking of moving. I am not suggesting that. Door knocking when you have a purpose is easy. The reception is also much better if you are there before or right after the sign goes up. People are curious.. It is sooo much easier to knock on a door when you have something interesting to tell them. As the local expert you are the perfect one to tell them. Most agents have a sign company install their sign and it takes 1-3 days to get it up. Follow the new listings everyday and go out immediately. You will usually get there before the sign is up.

I suggest that you call the owner and ask to preview the property immediately. Prepare a flyer that has info on the home.

After you see the home go directly and knock on the neighbors' doors. That way if anyone wants to visit about it, you will know the property. If they aren't home, leave a flyer and ask them to call you if they know anyone that might have interest in moving into the neighborhood.

Remember the goal is to add people to your database. You might find an occasional instant piece of business. However, you judge yourself by how many people are added to the database. Every time you meet someone that seems like someone you would like to work with when their time comes to move, add them to your database.

Let them know that you specialize in their area and that you will send them info from time to time about the market. It is perfect because you do not need to do the whole "May I have your name" thing. You are a Realtor. You know where they live and who they are. Perhaps on the last knock when the home closes ask for additional info for your file.

You need to have a touch system set up so that every new database person in those areas, gets special attention at first. I recommend to have at least 5 mailings plus your 3 door knocks (you aren't going to hold open on someone else's listing)

Immediately mail them a thank you after the first knock. Literally, immediately.

Have envelopes, stamps and stationery in your briefcase. Before you go back to the office mail them all a note. The same note that they each get after the first visit plus a personalized sentence. Drop it in a mailbox that day before the last pickup.

This is such a great business model. Every day you have purpose and know exactly what your 1st priority is. Plan your day around it. Assume that you will do your normal activities in the afternoon. Time block your mornings so that you consistently look for the new listings. Use a template that let's you build your flyer in minutes. Go look at the home before knocking on 10 to 20 neighbors. Everyday. Pick the best listings that come in everyday. The listing that you wish you had. The one next door will also be a good one someday.

Once you develop your system it will be smooth and you can be meeting people everyday. Some of which you will decide to put in your database and keep in touch with. Some of which you won't.

Pause and think for a minute how much business you could get if you personally had 200 listings a year and did all the things we are supposed to do when we get a listing. Just pick the top 200 listings that come into the market place and treat them as your own.

One last tip. When you start to get busy, you will be tempted to stop doing this. Don't stop. Time block that activity and have it be your thing that you do every morning. Show property and do your other follow up in the afternoon. If it pops up in your area, go see the neighbors. With time, the neighbors are people you have already door knocked, with a previous listing. Then you really are the expert.

One tip after the last tip: Read my chapter on "The Guess the Price Game." Combine these two chapters for your own Boomshackalacka, baby.

U.S.P.S. Me.S.P.S.

We are always looking for ways to be creative and thus memorable. It is important to build into your brand recognition development strategy, some unique and surprising moments. Images that are unexpected to our brain are more memorable. They also create moments of light conversation.

One way to do that is by creating your own custom postage stamps. You can make legal postage stamps that have any image that you choose on them. There are a few different websites that do that for you. Such as: zazzle.com, photostamps.com and pictureitpostage.com. You pay about twice the face value of the stamp. I last bought 20 stamps for $22.00 Cheap.

Here are some ways I suggest using them:

1. Regular old snail mail is more effective now than ever. People receive very little mail and tons of emails and text messages etc. very few hand written motes. Because of the impact of a hand written, mailed note is powerful right now. To increase the impact, have your recipient do a quick double take as they see you or your brand logo on the stamp. Some might be funny and some might be professional. Some might reinforce your brand or identity.

2. Take a picture of your client during the inspection in front of their new home. As a closing gift give them 20 stamps of that event. What an interesting way for them to mail out a few "we have moved" notes to friends and family. Most of those people will ask them where they got that incredible stamp. They will say from you.

3. If you have a group of clients that love the same sports team, take a picture of yourself in front of the stadium and create a stamp of that. They will love it when you mail them a quick note. This applies to any interest your clients might have. For about $20.00 you can create a special moment and light conversation with 20 of your biggest prospects. Some of the professional and college teams have their official logo already for purchase.

4. If you work a particular area, find what is identifiable with that area. When the locals see an image of ...... they all know that is right around the corner. Take those photos and make them into stamps. When you first have a contact with a new prospect, mail them a letter with that stamp. It reaffirms that you are a specialist in that area or you wouldn't have had a stamp made of you at that place. Do that several locations. Get some great images during the spring flowers. Every year you could use the same stamp during that season. Find seasonal images that are recognizable and be ready.

5. Follow social media for major events in your clients' lives. If for example they post a picture of their new baby, use that to buy them some stamps with their child on it. Give them a call first and ask if you can do something with their image as a gift. Don't tell them what but ask first if you do not have a close relationship. Most people will get a kick out of it. If it is an image of an adult that they posted online, go ahead and use the pic and surprise them.

8X8

There is a theory that states: there is one best way to do everything. One best way, to handle every recurring situation, in your business. Now your best way is going to be different than my best way. Decide what you feel is your perfect way to deal with something, then implement a system that makes sure that happens the exact same way every time.

As an example, you got referred to a nice couple that you have met with and they plan on selling in a few months. Because you really want this one you sit down and devise the perfect follow up plan for them. The perfect balance of phone calls with the perfect mailings that they will enjoy and find helpful. Now formalize that as the best way and do that every time the same situation comes up. Print out several copies of everything in your new system so they are ready when the situation arises. Be prepared so that the next time it takes you minutes and you already know what you are going to send and do.

I actually believe so strongly in the value of this that if I were your personal business coach, I would ask you to stop working until your systems are in place. Everything you do is something that happens over and over. Before you go back to work, decide how each of these situations should be handled and formalize that as your system that you automatically do, without any effort. It is already decided, printed out and organized.

29 Monsters 127

So what are some of the categories that you will need?
- --Just met. Into database. Not moving now.
- --FSBO
- --Maybe sell in a few months
- --Buyer just starting
- --Database person thinking of moving
- --Just went into escrow buyer
- --Just went into escrow seller
- --Just closed follow-up
- --Out of state seller or buyer
- --Met a potential advocate
- --Just got a referral from someone

As you implement your systems, you will immediately look very professional and will exceed client expectations.

The best part is that you do so with little effort. You have already decided when you will do what and put them in your calendar. You have designed your perfect combinations of mailings, emails, text messages, phone calls and in-person visits and how many days from today you will do each.

Do you think it would hurt your reputation with that client, if during the 30 day closing cycle, they also got:

- --- 2 page letter describing the process and what to expect,
- --- A helpful moving and packing hints flyer
- --- Forms and/or website to change their address with the post office,
- --- How to have a great garage sale info sheet
- --- List of the utility companies they will need
- ---- Rental truck tips, etc.

It helps you to exceed expectations if besides what you normally do, you have some things that go out automatically. Those extra touches that you designed, to make you look your best. Those touches that are now in a system that flows easily.

When you 1st meet someone, put them in your database and start sending them your newsletter or whatever your standard contact method is. In addition, you need 6-8 touches before you are cemented in their mind as "Oh, that's that Realtor person." When you first meet this person, enter them into the database and commit to the 8 additional upfront touches, that you have chosen ahead of time. Spread them out over the time frame that you have decided is best.

If it is a FSBO, you are pretty sure that they will list with someone within the next 2-3 weeks. So you don't send them something that goes out once a week for 8 weeks. No, you send something maybe every 3 days. Maybe your FSBO system is a 6x3. You have decided on 6 contacts in 3 weeks.

Notice I have been using the word contacts. You choose the pattern, but some of those contacts need to be in person and/or on the phone depending on the category.

I recommend a balance of mailing postcards and stamped envelopes w/ information inside. You know what did they call that… oh yeah, mail, that's right. A balance of phone calls, mailed letters, mailed postcards and emails..

I like postcards because it mixes it up. The letters can be serious. The postcard reminds them that you are an interesting person. It might be funny, relevant to their neighborhood or marketing. I also love postcards for sending copies of testimonials that I receive.

Usually in the letters, I would send items of value pertaining to the real estate world. I would probably send a postcard that is more clever or witty rather than informational. The postcard lightens things up but still has a point and reminds them of you. The letter is something they might think has value and it will enhance your image as a pro.

Or…… any combination you choose ahead of time that is perfect and comfortable, for you. Just have it be your best and then duplicate it over and over.

I believe that often times the first touch, after you have just met a person, whether you met a seller at his house or met a new buyer at a showing, be handwritten. Take with you in your briefcase some of the stationery for this 1st note and pull over and write it immediately. As you drive down the road, hit a mailbox and mail it before they pick up that day's mail.

It is so impressive when the prospect gets the card the next day. They can't believe it came so fast and that helps you to stand out. You might also consider having the first touch be a text. It should come a couple minutes after you leave them and should say something like " It was great to meet you. Your daughter is the cutest ever. Made my day. I will get back to you tomorrow with the info your requested. " or "thank you for the chance to visit with the 2 of you about selling your home. I really enjoyed it. I will see you tomorrow at 3:00"

Design a specific set of 8 touches that you will do for each category. Address and stamp the touches when you get back. Enter into your calendar the future phone call. You are done. Have it all set up so it takes just a few minutes and the system is in place, Then do your normal follow up and…

Boomshackalacka, hero baby….

3 Rituals for Success

I'd like to talk about three, 5 minute Rituals, that if implemented into a real estate agent's life, assures consistent improvement in their income as well as in their personal sales skills.

Whatever you do, don't stop any of the rest of what you are doing. Do not stop all of your prospecting and follow-up activities. I am not suggesting that 15 minutes a day is all you need to do... come on now, don't even think about it.

BUT... if you want a boost in your income, I have an easy answer.

The three, 5 minute time frames, when we do our rituals are:

First 5 minutes of your workday
5 minutes before a big appointment
5 minutes after the big appointment

First 5 Minutes of the Work Day

I love to read great books. Literally, not on a device, just printed out and I hold it, in my hands. That allows me to highlight and dog ear pages and keeps me from sucking my thumb.

There are several good ones that talk of how we need to find, our Big Why. We need to have a monster goal that would "change lives for the better," kind of goal. Really imagine your best life you could have and most fulfilling contributions we could make, to the world and to your family. What would be an off the charts, fulfilling life for you? Identify your BIG WHY and what would be a huge goal and life, for you to have. The thing, that would excite us everyday to work on. The thing, we would talk someone's ear off about.

Then we work backwards and figure things we could do in the short term, which would point the nose of our ship in that direction. Make a list of little things you would need to do to assure that you are slowly headed that direction. Towards Your One Big Why Purposeful Thing...

Now here comes the Ritual. Every morning, for the first 5 minutes if needed, 15 seconds if not needed, when you get to the office, decide what is the one thing, just one little thing, you could do today to continue down the path towards your biggest goal. Got it? Just one thing, that is a step towards a really big life. One, so that we never go a full day, and do nothing (aka: no-thing), towards our biggest ambition.

Commit to doing just one thing today and then time block it into your schedule. Literally, write in your schedule or calendar, when you're going to do it. Then, go about your day and do what you need to do. Don't move that appointment. Treat it like your number one most important thing, to accomplish today. Everyday do one thing that takes you, with baby steps, towards your dream.

5 minutes before a BIG appointment

So often in our career, we are juggling many balls at once. We are fiercely proud of the fact that we talked on the phone and solved a few problems, while driving to our next appointment. We get there and just go in and wing it, because we are pros. But

3 Rituals for Success

really, we are a little distracted and have a million things on our mind. We're more likely to miss that point, we meant to bring up, when we go straight from one task to an important task.

I propose, that before you go inside, that you sit in a quiet place and totally clear your mind. Do a mini version of a meditation and focus on your breathing and a lack of thoughts. Force your mind to think of nothing, except the monitoring of your breathing.

Author of The Charisma Myth, Olivia Fox Cabane, tells us that before we speak or sell or present, we should stop and put our minds in a place of gratitude and love and acceptance. It will show in our eyes and the client will feel it. We need to remind ourselves that the person we are about to meet is a good human and that, skip the whole commission thing, we would really like to help them and have a positive effect on their lives. I recom-mend that before any big appointment or important event, you stop and either read or say to yourself, an affirmation similar to the one, I have written here. It should go some-thing like:

--I am looking forward to seeing _____ today. It is a gift that I get this opportunity to help them. One of the great things about this world, is how everyone is so unique and different, from each other. I have not walked a mile in my clients' shoes, but I know their path, was different than mine. Their childhood, relationships and work experiences, all influenced them to be who they are. Please, help me to not judge them, if they react differ-ently than I would. My life has been different than theirs. I am no better than they are and God loves them, just as much, as God loves me. I hope that as they go forward, that they have a fabulous life, which gets better and better.

I accept _____ for who he is and will give 100% of my attention to him. If I really focus on every word he says, I know I will better understand and know him. If I find my mind wandering, I will bring it back, so that he will know I am really listening and that I care about him, because I do.

29 Monsters

I can see myself being very relaxed and profess-ional. This is a very comfortable conversation for me. I will say less and have pauses before my speaking, to give time to reflect. I am the best and my product is the best for them and I am very fortunate to be here, regardless of the outcome. I am grateful for an opportunity to share my skills and be the best agent for _____ to work with. I am very fortunate to have a job that allows me to help so many people. I am thankful that I have been given the natural skills, to be able to be in the moment and to have empathy for all people. I calmly understand the words I should use, that will help them realize that I really am the real estate agent for them.

Got it? Center yourself and bring your focus in on them, while keeping in mind, that you come from a place of gratitude and acceptance. It doesn't mean we give up and don't close. It means we commit to understanding and respecting them. Their opinions are valid and if I had lived in their shoes, I might think the same.

We still try and help them and we close them, if we know we are the right one for them. But we do so with respect. When you reach that place of calm gratitude and confidence, stop and review your notes before you go in. Make sure you cover each point and deliver your message in the order that you designed, without getting side tracked.

5 Minutes after the BIG appt.

In the sports world, all of the greatest athletes have a post game analysis. They watch tape of their performance and evaluate what they did well and what could be improved. What you may not realize is that many of the Monster Salespeople, do the same thing. Many of the big team leaders do the same thing with their team members.

3 Rituals for Success

**The road to constant improvement,
travels through the place of continuous self-analysis,
and the tweaking of our words, actions, and our responses.**

    It doesn't do us any good, to leave and think that the seller is a bum and stupid, because he chose a different option. That is totally outward centered, and feels good to some of us to place blame elsewhere. If we want to improve our closing ratio and have more success in the future, we should stop immediately after our appointment, while it is still fresh in our minds. Ask ourselves, what did we do great. Write it down, to make sure you emphasize that segment in the future.

    Just as important of course, is what could we have done differently, or better. How could we handle that situation differently, next time. Do we need to develop a new script for that repeating objection? Write it down. Contemplate how you might continue on your path, of consistent personal growth and higher closing ratios.

    This is meant to become a habit that we form and do after every major appointment, whether it was a great one and we got the business, or we failed and did not get the business. That 5 minute time frame, will become invaluable to you, in identifying what is needed, to make sure we win more often.

    Sounds easy, doesn't it? Duh, it is easy. Three times a day, take 15 seconds to 5 minutes, and change your career. Really, change your life.

    1st Ritual.. Can you imagine how much MORE LIKELY you are to achieve your greatest and wildest dream if you actually take some step in that direction everyday and do at least one thing?

    2nd Ritual.. Can you imagine how much better some of your appointments will be, if we don't just race in, coming straight from being on a phone call, solving problems on a different transaction? Our attention will be refocused and our emotions will be brought in check, so that we can be 100% present, with the client that is in front of us. They will feel it.

3rd Ritual, we can't improve our closing ratio if we keep doing the same thing we did last time. The only way to improve, is to stop and reflect on what was fabulous and in what area, we would like to have a do-over. Because in life as a salesperson, we really do get a ton of do-overs… just not on the client we just lost.

We will have the same or similar situation, come up again and again. That, is our do-over, to commit to ourselves to handle things slightly differently next time we get the similar opportunity.

I'm feeling that is worth a BOOYAH.

Hello I am a Realtor

Hello I am a Realtor
and I thought I'd let you know
that your neighbor has just listed
and I thought you might say "Whoa."

And though it's not my listing
this neighborhood is mine.
Of course I wish I had it
but you won't hear me whine.

The reason I have come here
and knocked upon your door
is I can handle much more business.
Please sir, give me some more.

There's a funny thing that happens
when someone lists their home.
Their neighbors soon start talking
That's why I wrote this poem

They sit and talk about it
and think that they should move.
They'd like an extra bedroom
and they'd like an extra loo.

So next thing that I know
another one's for sale.
Now I missed two listings
And all I can say is Hale.

I hate it when that happens.
So that is why I'm here.
To see if you are one of those
and you'd like outa here.

So if you need a Realtor
A good one, not a slob
your neighbors will all tell you
It's simple, just choose Bob.

I promise to work hard for you
and always tell the truth.
Sometimes my humor's kind of weird
but it never gets uncouth.

But when it's time for moving day
I don't lift or climb up ladders.
I just cover all the details.
Why? You know, cuzitmatters.

You Are NOT a Realtor

I am going to talk about a subject that is near and dear to my heart. Many of you are Realtors. Not me. I used to be a Realtor and I made more money than most. When I stopped being a real estate agent, is when the big bucks kicked in.

I know you were all very proud of yourself when you got your license and became a real estate sales-person. I got the memo because it was really quite newsworthy. Really, congratulations. That is quite a feat. It made me joyous hearing of it because what the world really needs, is one more stinking Realtor. There really is quite a shortage of real estate agents and I understand why. The years of dedication and advanced degrees required to get that license are just too much to ask of most people, in order to get that rare and coveted real estate sales person license.

Like for me as an example, my neighbor is a Realtor, my aunt Matilda's boyfriend is a part time agent, my golfing buddy was a Realtor for awhile and my cousin tells me he is thinking he'd be a good one but isn't sure if he wants to or not. He does know that of course he would be good at this job. I mean how much does it take, right?

I used to be a salesperson. I used to be proud of my profession and now I am embarrassed. If someone called me a salesman at a party, I would hang my head and shrink home, with my tail between my legs. Another stinking salesperson. I used to be.... You. Bummer.

But, noooo. Dignity regained... I have evolved from Neanderthal Man to Sales Man to Business Man... er... uh.... Owner. Yeah, that's the ticket... I meant Business Owner. When I stopped being a sales person and became a business owner, my income skyrocketed. I got better control of my life and of my time, and geometrically multiplied the net. You know, that spread between revenue and expenses. If you want to be successful, as a salesperson,

I suggest you not be a salesperson.

Be a business owner.

When I made the transition, I went from B-O-B the Realtor to B-O-B the CEO, CFO and sales manager, of the Bob Bloom Real Estate Sales Company. For the first time, I stopped trying to sell stuff and decided to run a business, my business. Skip the Rodney deal and treat yourself and your career, with respect. Treat the business side of your life, as a business.

That is kind of a cute statement. I love cute stuff. It sells books. However, what does that really mean? What do successful business owners do?

Running a business of any size, assumes growth and thus hiring employees. No one is about to start hiring people and letting them answer the phone, interact with customers or make any decisions, flying by the seat of their pants. The business owner is going to teach them exactly the words to use and the procedures to follow.

For you see, there is:

ONE & ONE ONLY, BEST WAY

to handle every situation that might come up. Similar situations repeat themselves, over and over, within your business context. Owners analyze each small act in their business, and decide the best way to handle it. (O.K. you naysayer, critical types…. I can hear you thinking… uh, uh.. there are a million different scenarios and everyone might handle it their way, and blah…blah…blah. You are wrong. Most scenarios we run across, are scenarios that

You are NOT a Realtor

we will tend to run across. Of course, your best way, is different than mine. However, we need to, as a business owner would, stop and decide what is the best way we should handle these repeating situations.)

Every business owner has certain protocols, dress codes, procedures and policies. As they grow, they must formalize these procedures, so all may adhere. At that point, they need to write them down, so that they are standard. From time to time, some would be changed, because a better way has been discovered. Then all will follow the new guidelines. When they do this, it forces the owner to really decide the best way, to do each thing.

Every business owner wants their image to be consistent.

Every business owner holds board meetings. They set aside time, to work on their business, instead of just in their business. At the board meeting, the owner looks at bigger picture game plans and strategies. This is the time to choose long term direction, make corrections, analyze the efficacy of your marketing, dream of that perfect niche to develop, decide which clients to dump and which to pursue, and basically, not be so bogged down in the current, that you lose sight of the future.

I have a weekly board meeting. It takes me less than an hour. I turn off phones, put my feet up on the desk, (shoeless) and pull out my laptop. I keep a running document, with all my Board Meeting thoughts. This is the time to dream big and create strategies that would have career changing endings. A weekly board meeting keeps us on track.

Monsters

Every business owner has scripts and has decided the best way to answer the phone, greet customers, handle objections and solve problems. The best salespeople, all use scripts. They may be scripts that sound a dash different, each time, but they always follow the same multi-step process, to lead the client correctly. Thus many of the words, are exact every time. They do this, so that they don't have to think about it and because they took the time to analyze their single best way to handle repeat objections or problems. Never again, leave an appointment and think to yourself, "I wish I would have said such and such." Never again, feel guilty or anxious, about whether or not you lost that piece of business, because you didn't follow-up as good as you do sometimes. Do it the same every time.

Every business owner analyzes the value of each employee and each activity, that person does. They have to. They need to know, what bang they are getting for their buck, in each area. Whether it is the cost of marketing or the cost of time, what is the return on that investment?

Every business owner delegates. They figure out what they are best at and focus on those things. That also means, that the things that they are not good at, or things, that someone who gets paid less, can do, they pass off. One way to grow, is to make more per hour. Dump the low value stuff and spend most of your energy, where you create the most value, for your company. As a business owner, would you have your Rock Star saleswoman, helping out in the mailroom, a few hours per day?

Every business owner has client touch systems and makes decisions, about how best to "farm," his past clients. He would never send a "thank you for meeting me" note, if it didn't conform to the pre-thought out, perfect way, to say, thank you. Yes, the middle paragraph would vary, because that is where we add the personal stuff. However, each and every time, an employee sends a thank you, after a first meeting, it would cover three main points that the owner has decided, are the perfect things to cover. They are the highest and best practices for that event. The owner might then make the employee, enter that contact into an automatic follow-up system. That takes the human error and whimsy, out of each follow up. Every client gets handled the same way, depending on the category that they fit into.

When I discuss database development, I say that I believe, if you do not have specific follow-up systems in place, for every type of client and every recurring situation you run across…..

STOP WORKING.

Truly. Stop everything and design your systems. It takes too long to think about, what to write and what follow up you should do. Your time is better spent, designing how you will handle every situation, if you were your best. Then build your business protocols that commit to protecting that system of consistency.

Sorry gang, but the world has enough salespeople, perhaps a couple extra. However, the world never has enough good business owners. Running your business, as a business, keeps you on track and gives you true purpose. Purposeful people are more successful. They have a clear direction that leads them where they chose. They have a better grasp, on the value of their time and the return, on both their time and their marketing dollars.

That has to beat being a real estate salesperson, eh?

Weekly Goals

Thought I would introduce you to a topic, that you most likely have never heard anything about... Goal setting. O.K., some of you may have some thoughts on that. Here is one of mine.

There is much attention given to the topic of establishing and meeting daily goals. The whole "time blocking" and daily commitments to your, "get 'er done" list. Best laid plans..... For many of us, things beyond our control pop up and need our immediate attention. Yes, we need to learn to limit or delegate those, but still, it happens. We have no chance of doing all of the things we committed to do, today.

When that does happen, you are just another lousy, stinking failure. You made a commitment 9 hours ago and couldn't even keep your word, to yourself, for one day. Loser!   Really. If we have a specific, "To Do Today" list that we created with much thought and commitment, and then we don't do it, our brain remembers. It remembers that you made a commitment and didn't meet it, but that's O.K. cuz...... it happens. No big deal.

It is a huge deal. If we train ourselves to make a commitment to ourself, and it is alright to break it, we lower our personal integrity. We get used to not doing, what we said we would. Our subconscious knows, that we don't have to do all that stuff, just make a good list and try. When we have many things on our "To Do Today" list, we fail more often.

I love the "Weekly To Do" list, as well as a shorter, daily commitment list. There are always things, that need to get done today, but many of our activities are meant to build our business and just need to get done over and over, every week.

I believe we lose integrity to ourselves, and our word becomes meaningless, if not kept. You can't fake it with your own mind. You either did what you committed to do, or did not.

Weekly Goals

So what should our weekly goals be? They should always be "activity" goals, and never sales goals. We can not control when we get a sale or when we get the signed paperwork. Sometimes we will have huge months and sometimes, it seems like nothing is coming together. If our goal is to have 4 sales and we have 3, then we are a failure and the emotional roller coaster rolls on.

We should not set ourselves up for failure, by having goals that we can not control. The only thing we can control for sure, is what we do. Our activities.

Internalize that for a second. If at the end of the week, your honey asks, "How was your week?" the answer is "Fabulous," even though you didn't make one sale. When we, and more importantly, those around us, think we judge ourselves by short-term results, meaning sales, it is crippling. If it is about sales, then my week sucked and my mother-in-law was right. I'm a loser. Zero sales all week. Back to flippin' burgers.

But as we teach ourselves and our support system, that we are building a Monster Career, and am committed to do those activities that get me there, every week....

Boomshackalacka, Baby. I had a fabulous week, and met all my goals. I am on my way. Are you horny?

I believe this is important. The first time, your spouse or dad, asks "How was your week, did you sell anything,?" we need to set the ground rules and explain what we are doing. We explain what activities are important to us to build a career. Then in the future dad will ask, "Did you get your five new database folks this week, boy?" Our weekly goals, should be to do those things that assure we will always get more than our share. That is some-thing we have complete control over.

Those weekly activities would include things like:

Prospecting: We all need to continue to prospect, whether that is for new clients, or new sales out of our existing client base. I used to commit to adding 5 people to my database every week, even if they were not buyers, currently. Many would set prospecting goals, as a number of phone calls/contacts or hours spent per week.

Current Business: Eventually you will have many clients at a time. I commit to having at least one contact with each of those, every week. Sometimes, there is nothing to talk about and so we don't have a single communication all week, with our most current clients. Not a good idea. If by Friday, you have not had a purpose to touch in, find one or call and say "nothing to say this week, but I wanted to see if you need anything from me, before the week is over?"

Database Development: Many of us have past clients, that we seldom speak to. They may be a solid core, of our referral business, but it gets harder to touch in if there is no real purpose. Some of these end up slipping into the "never talk to" category. On any given week, it is not urgent and you are busy.

I suggest, you create a list of them and call X number, per week. Just a few, but be consistent. It will save you business that eventually will be vulnerable. It will force you to do what makes your life easier. Nurturing people that like you. You never know when the referrals will come but they do not come without keeping in front of these folks from time to time.

Self Improvement: Most of the monster performers, practice their scripts weekly. They change and adapt them, but even after years of selling, they keep sharp, with weekly practice. It actually surprised me how many of the best agents that I was sure knew their scripts backwards and forward, still practice them. Several do so while driving to an appointment.

Weekly Goals

Some of us, could earn designations within our field that would enhance our image and knowledge, I will be honest. There was a huge disparity on how the monsters feel about this. More than half could care less because their business is database or marketing driven.

They didn't think anyone cared. Several did believe in them greatly. I think especially if you choose to develop commercial or luxury niches they are most helpful. This also, is where you commit to reading X # of chapters, in a self-improvement type book

Your Future: Some of you have dreams of being something else, or starting something new, someday. Never let a week go by, that you don't do something, to that end.

Board Meeting: I talk about this elsewhere, but this is always on my weekly list. I put my feet up and spend some uninterrupted time, thinking Big Picture thoughts, about my business.

Your Health: It is hard to get to the gym some days, but there is no excuse why we can't make it, X times per week. I include meditation and my affirmations, in my health section and commit to X times per week. I would include any spiritual development, in this category.

Your Personal Life: Radical thought, but it takes more than work, to be fulfilled. Make sure a week never slips by, that you let your loved ones be ignored. Think of ways to make the family time you have, be special.

Don't ignore the fact that you need to be you and express yourself, in a hobby or activity that is uniquely you.

Monsters

Referrals: Many of us get great value, from receiving referrals. Many of us, seldom ask for one. Make it a weekly habit, to at least ask for a referral, X# of times.

Other: Many experts believe, you should write hand written thank you notes, for a bigger impact. You might commit, to writing 5 per week.

If you have figured out the value of a gratitude journal, write your commitment here.

Got the idea? Decide which activities are critical, if you are going to have a great year, as well as a great career and track them. I actually print this list out and look at it, throughout the day. I literally put a check in each box, as I do one of the items. It really keeps me on track to know what I need to do and feels great when I have done them. I may have some crazy individual days, but by the end of the week, they all get done.

Trivia Quiz

I love this concept. I love it because it is fun and I like fun. Plus I have learned that people like to work with fun people. People work with a real estate agent that they like and people like fun people.

In addition it allows me to be unique and stand out in the crowd. It shows my creative side and clients seem to think that creative people might bring creative marketing to the table for their home. But the best part is, we are always trying to prove we are the local expert. We know everything about the local market. How fun to do an activity that helps you learn odd things about your target market and accents that fact, to the people you are targeting.

Create several, one page trivia games about the local area. Find out about the history, the early settlers, a famous politician, celebrity or sports figure. Then create a multiple-choice quiz, around that info. Make sure that your name is always one of the choices. It continually reinforces who you are and allows you to have fun with it.

Throw some choices that sound like they might be true and have some that nonsensical. Make sure they can get some right and hopefully be tricked by a couple.

I use them as part of my touch system. When I add a new person to my database, they get 8 touches from me in the first 8 weeks. Some show I am very professional, some are testimonials and this one is meant to make me human. You know, a fun guy.

I don't have prizes but you could. You just would have to be there at the time they answer because Mr. Google knows all the correct answers.

My intention is to have the client learn something about the area that I am the professional in. I want them to say, "Wow, I didn't know that" and to chuckle.

Monsters

I recommend that you create one for the City and county that you live in. In addition create separate trivia quizzes for each identifiable area that you work in. If there is not enough info for that area to find 4 or 5 questions, then fill in the blanks with those you have for the city or county. Then use it forever, as one of your touch points for your clients. Play the game with every new buyer. Use one that covers the area they are looking in. If possible break down a question or two that is subdivision specific such as: Who first homesteaded the property that we call Ashley Heights today? That allows you to hone in on any target market that you want to proclaim, that you are the expert of. It becomes easy to quickly recall and have data that makes you look like you really know more than they do, about their neighborhood. It only takes one or two specific questions and fill in the rest with some of your general area quizzes.

Here are a few examples.

How did Lady Island get its name?

1- Named by the original owner of Lady's Saloon in 1860
2- Named after a very manly early settler with the misfortune to have "Lady" as his first name.
3- Lady was famous explorer Lewis Bloom's dog's name. Her friend was a tramp.
4- Lady Bird Johnson camped out there once.

Trivia Quiz

The term "Lacamas" comes from:

    A. The local native American tribe, named by Lewis & Clark
    B. The French version of "veni, vidi, vici" meaning "he did it all"
    C. The Camas lily tuber eaten by local natives
    D. Bob Bloom's middle name, is "Lacamas"

The first African American to settle in the area was:

    A. George Bush
    B. Bubba Bloom (Bob's great, great grandfather)
    C. Samuel Jackson
    D. Ronald Reagan

(You want to know something funny? The answer is George Bush.)

The area's first permanent resident, Richard Ough, married:

    A. Wealthy Bostonian, Rose Bloom, in an arranged marriage
    B. A Native American lady named White Wing
    C. His sister, Rough Ough
    D. Sacajawea

Trivia Quiz 2.0

Another way your Trivia Quizzes can be used, is as a database development tool. Have a monthly quiz that you email to your database. Make it clear that you are not offended if they opt out. Some won't want to receive it and you do not want to get blocked. Many will love it and look forward to it. Make the questions fun and everybody likes to hit the freebie drawing.

Make the quiz easy enough that many will succeed. Assume that many have the right answers because they will do a quick search. That is OK because you are going to have a drawing of all the winners.

Have it be the same day of the month so they get used to it. I would video the drawing and make it fun. It is very easy to turn that into a private Youtube video. Then send them the link to that video with the results so no one thinks you cheated,

I would have a dinner out and then some car washes or lottery tickets or…. Most restaurants have built in to their budget, free dinners where they get some exposure. They eat this up. If you have a database of homeowners, many within the restaurant's target market, you will easily get free dinners to offer.

We always talk about having a "Pop by" with some of our best database clients. Few of us do that. This is an easy way to do so. Drop off the prize to them. Sometimes it will be a great way to have a short re-connect for a few minutes. Sometimes they will have time and invite you in. Then you get to a deeper level. Sometimes you will mail it or drop it under the mat if it is in anyway inconvenient for the client.

It is a fabulous idea to force yourself to phone the top 100 of your clients and ask their permission. Another thing many of us do less than we know we should, is phone our database. It is hard. This idea gives you purpose to your call. A phone call with

Trivia Quiz

purpose is easy to make. You look interesting, clever or crazy to them as you explain what you are doing. Then you show respect and ask permission. It might make you look creative. It might open a light-hearted conversation with your chosen few.

That also means that at the beginning, there isn't everybody yet and that increases the odds, for your favorite prospects. After you get all called that you are going to call, send an introductory email to the rest of your database. Of course, I was supposed to say to phone the entire database but I know you won't. Good idea but when we start doing that calling thing, we get business and then we get busy and stop calling…

Keep any hint of sales away from it. Do not make it part of some newsletter or have a couple new listings with the quiz. If you do, you will eventually be blocked by many. Keep it short and sweet with a side order of clever.

BIG GROUPS=BIG BUCKS

    I would like to talk about something, that is seldom done by salespeople or most companies. Something that uses your time very efficiently. This idea sets you apart, as a unique and value adding person. It creates synergy by bringing together your clients under one roof and is just down right cool.
    That is, putting on large, group meetings, of interest. If you currently, never bring together any clients, then a group of 2 is big, as well.
    What if you found reasons, to create gatherings that people would find interesting, informative and enhance your image.

Why

Build deeper relationships in a relaxed setting
Synergy of your clients talking together about you
Show charisma, when stand up and briefly speak
Look like a leader, if you are in control of the Setting

    One great idea is to put on a candidates night. Every election season, the candidates are desperately looking for ways to get in front of voters. Many voters welcome a chance to see their choices live, and ask them questions. Call a couple candidates to pick a date. If one is available, then they all will be, because they travel the same circuit and are busy the same nights. If their competitor is going to be there, trust me, they will try very hard to be available.

BIG GROUPS =BIG BUCKS

Invite your entire database. If that does not fill a room, let the paper know and they will publicize it. Have people write down questions they would like asked, of particular candidates or positions. In order to have their question asked, they must include their name. That allows you the chance to call them back and thank them, for their involvement. Let each candidate speak for 3-5 minutes. Have someone be the timer, whom raises a card, when time is up. After they have spoken, have a Q & A period, where you either read the questions or you let people come up, and ask their question.

Don't turn it into a big marketing campaign for you. The goal is to add value to your folks and to increase your presence, in the community, without looking too obvious about it.

Perhaps at the beginning of tax season, give a free tax tips seminar. You will easily be able to find an accountant, that would like the publicity and clients that are appreciative to listen. Make sure the accountant you choose, has some speaking skills. He/she is accountant, after all.

The whole gluten free thing has become a major topic and many people are still learning about it. Find a couple of experts that can give research data, recipes and lifestyle tips. The people that do come, will be very appreciative. Find a way to capture the names of who came and follow up to see if there is any more info on the topic, you can get them.

Consider Investment Advice night, where you have a financial advisor, a stockbroker, an accountant and someone who can talk about the local real estate opportunities. Give each a few minutes to talk and have a Q & A period.

When a new bridge or freeway ramp is going in, invite the local politicians or government employee that knows about it, as well as the construction company foreman and educate people, about the topic.

Monsters

Find a location where you can have a large group of football fans come together. When the Super Bowl or the local college team, has a big game, be party central and create a monster, fun party. (no alcohol unless you hold it at a bar where someone else has the liability) Get a table and bring together a few clients that share the same passion for the home team, at the sports bar.

In the spring you could easily find a nursery owner that would come and bring a couple experts with him, to speak about gardening tips.

People go nuts trying to help their kids get an advantage, in the sport of their choice. Why not gather together a couple coaches and put on a free, kids soccer, basketball or whatever clinic? You could help out or you could mingle with parents, while it went on.

Many towns have a local parade that you can participate in, for free. Find a flat bed truck and decorate it up a bit. Invite your clients' kids to ride on it and give them bags of candy to throw.

As fishing season approaches, hold a fly-casting or???? seminar, for the fisherman.

Our company, has rented out a whole theater for our clients, thrown a Back to School Carnival, where all kids got free school supplies and A Christmas Craft Fair, where they made free crafts with help from elves and a pic with the Real Santa. Really, it might be. This guy was great.

Our clients look forward to our annual events.

When you have free, "concerts in the park," in your area, go down early and set up 20 chairs, that you
have reserved for your clients. You can buy lawn chairs for about $6.00. You could have 20 of them for $120.00. In my area, they hold a summer series and you could use those same chairs, 8 or 9 times. For a few bucks you
could bring together people, that you'd like to get to know better, 8 or 9 times. Incredible value for the money.

BIG GROUPS =BIG BUCKS

There are possibilities of cooking tips for vegetarians, study or behavioral tips for parents with youngsters, college prep classes and on and on. Whatever would be an interesting topic, for some segment of your clients and prospects, is good. It also works well, when you have one on a topic, that you are passionate about, but not necessary.

Anytime that we can bring together a chosen group of our raving fans, all benefit. The clients that like you will talk about you to whomever they end up sitting by. They all will get a chance to talk behind your back about you. They will re-enforce to each other that you are the best... Cool.

Big groups will increase the number of referrals that you receive from your core group.

It gives you purpose to communicate with your entire current database and remind them that you are a professional and still around. It is an easy and non-offensive touch.

Because you will encourage your clients to bring a friend that has interest in the topic, you will add to your database.

I refer to this, as **a Boomshackalacka** moment.

Coming Soon

In a market where there is very little inventory, buyers chase and chase to be the first one to see a new listing. In a market where they have made multiple offers and been too late on a couple others, first is the goal.

In a market where sellers get offers the first day, they tend to wonder if they sold too soon or too cheap. They accepted an offer before much of the market even had time to be aware of their beautiful home.

The answer in both cases is for the real estate agent to employ the "Coming Soon" strategy.

Run ads with the "Coming Soon" headline. Buy signs and sign riders with the same message. Buyers will call and they will give you their name and phone number. It is a fabulous way to get a plethora of buyers. Great for teams or agents that like buyers.

The strategy is also a great listing tool. Let the sellers know that you want to make sure they get the greatest exposure and highest price possible. You want to make sure that every possible buyer has time to be aware of it. That will give them the confidence to end the bidding war and accept an offer, once their listing is live on the market.

Obviously we represent the seller and need to do so. I am not talking about a way for you to double dip on a transaction because you are the insider. You need to have the listing go active on your local multiple listing service and make it available to all agents and buyers. During your pre-list stage, it is mandatory that you cooperate with all agents that call. Be upfront and let them know exactly when the home will be listed and at what price etc.

I am talking about being ethical. I mean to represent the seller better because of the additional exposure. I intend to meet

Coming Soon

lots of buyers and have a real reason for them to call me. Buyers usually don't need to call me because any home I advertise, they can look up on the internet. "Coming Soon" homes, require they call me.

I would run the campaign for a week before the listing date. You can not let buyers into the home until it is active on MLS. You can share info. and set a time to show it, when it is available. I suggest that the home be active for at least a couple days to make sure all is fair.

What a win/win. Better for seller, buyers and you.

Boomshackalacka

I have a story I'd like to tell.
About two agents and one did well.

Both of them they had the look
and both had the social skill.
One wallowed in the valley
and one atop the hill.

What could be the difference?
Was it pre-destined fate?
One was always starving
the other, a full plate.

Pre-destiny, is nonsense.
We choose who we will be.
Some have no direction.
Some plan their destiny.

They do it by the little things
that others tend to skip.
Some say that they just wing it,
while some work on their script.

Tale of 2 Agents

I know that there are many men
that work hard day and night.
But they travel round in circles
cuz they have no goal in sight

Some folks when they are busy
they just focus on today.
They never seem to get ahead
success is kept at bay.

I say that they can't get there
if they don't know where there, is.
Round and round and round they go
in their life and in their biz.

To me it sounds a bit bizarre.
They are crazy as mad hatters.
Why should they do the little things?
I say "cuzitmatters."

Tell 'em You're Great

Our clients tend to think that we are overpaid. We are those high commission folks, that drive fancy cars, take clients to lunch, golf and get to look at cool houses.. We even get out of the office and get to drive around while others are chained to a desk.

All that the client sees, is us open a few doors, gloss over some paperwork and get paid a bunch. It looks fun. Why do you think everyone thinks they want to be a real estate agent.... Before they try it?

The reason is, that we make it look too easy. They don't see, what we really do and have no idea, what hoops we jumped through and the genius, that we exhibited...... unless, we tell 'em.

Countless Realtors, after a difficult negotiation, call their client and say, "Congratulations. You got the home."

What A Waste

If you perform a miracle, just as important, if you don't, let your client know how hard you worked for them and what a hero you are. Before you tell 'em the good news, walk them through a dramatic story. How you created magic and got them what they desired. A real miracle worker & frankly, they should feel lucky to work with you. The Magic Man or Woman, as it so may be.

You may think that the way we deserve a big fee, is if we have value, beyond price. You would be wrong.

The way we deserve a Monster fee or undying loyalty, is if the client REALIZES, we have great value. Who cares what we do, if no one knows and they assume, that it was no big deal.

If we got them the home of their dreams or theirs sold at top dollar, they will think it is no big deal, if we act like, it was no big deal.

Tell 'em You're Great

As a Realtor you might say something like:

"OMG, that seller is a tough one. He knows he has great property and there is a lot of interest, from other buyers. The listing agent told me, she expected more offers by tomorrow, so I pulled in a favor and got Susie, who I have known for years, to push it through tonight. I feel very fortunate that I have worked with this agent so many times, over the years and she said she knew, if I was involved that it was a solid deal, so she left her kids soccer game early, for you.

By the time she got back to her office, she already had another offer. I don't know if it was better or worse, but I am so glad I have a good reputation, with this agent and yes, congratulations, we got your home, by minutes. What a great home. I am so glad we snuck in before all the competition created a bidding war, that I really wanted to avoid for you guys.

Congratulations."

Now your client thinks you are a hero. If you would have called and said "we got it", they would have thought to themselves, we should have offered lower. Feel that difference. Hmmm, they accepted the offer. No big deal, I must not have negotiated well enough or Whoa... I am so lucky, I picked El Bobbo as my Realtor.

Don't over do it, but realize that this is not just for the big things. If you let them know that it was **not** just standard and that you care about them enough, to go the extra mile, they will appreciate you more. They will feel better about paying a large fee if they know how hard you worked and how skillful you were. They will only know that, if you tell 'em.

They will be more appreciative and thus loyal. Trust me, if you don't tell 'em you're great, no one will.

In the "one last thought" category: when a customer thanks you, never say no big deal or shut them off early. Let them go on, until they stop and then acknowledge that, this was a tough one and you were really glad for the outcome and…. You're welcome.

In the 'thought after the last thought,' category: When someone is thanking you and thinks you are the best, it might be the right time to say:

"You are welcome, do you happen to know of anyone else that might benefit from the way that I work?"

Teams: When & Why

I would like to share the reasons these monster real estate agents considered developing a team as they grow. The whole team leader thing is not for everybody and you don't have to have a team to do very well in this business. Usually the Realtors that end up building a team, do so for one of 4 reasons:

Greater Income
Better Control over their Life
Improve slipping Service Levels
Build a Saleable Asset

But first lets take a look at why you might not want to have a team. For some of you that list might be longer. For example:

Not Cut Out for Management
Satisfied with Current Income
Time Control Not an Issue

Being satisfied with one's current income is not a put down in anyway. The beauty of this business is that it offers so many different opportunities. There is one that fits each of us.

Here are the 4 most common reasons why agents decide the benefit, outweighs the hassle:

Greater Income

The most common reason I see as to why an agent developed their team is because they want to get to a higher level than they can do on their own. They are maxed out in their time and energy, so there income is maxed as well.

Often it is an agent that is doing 30-50 transactions a year and knows they could do more. More if there were just more hours in the day. This same agent probably is thinking that they are more valuable in front of people than doing the paperwork or stamping the monthly newsletter. There becomes a point where it is not physically possible to take your business to any higher level without the use of leverage.

You need to refine what you do into a written system that is easy to follow and then pass off those duties to someone you pay hourly. The first key to growth is to hire an administrative assistant and then go do what is the most valuable use of your time.

Better Control of Their Life

This same agent that is selling quite a few houses every year, might be burning out. It seems like she can never get a whole weekend off with her family. He feels stressed saying no to a client that wants to look at a house because you promised your spouse that you would have a quiet dinner together tonight.

You might not have noticed, but though I can name more advantages to being in this business, it's not always the perfect job. It can get in the way of having fun sometimes and I like fun…

Teams: When & Why

That is the second most popular thing we hear from team leaders. They got their life back. They hire a buyer's agent to work with any leads generated by your marketing, including the sign calls. You might choose to keep your repeat clients and friends for yourself. Or they hire an agent that shares duties on your listings. One where you do the initial interview and the negotiations when there is an offer, but your listing specialist does everything else and will be in contact with the seller regularly.

Improve Service Levels

Sometimes as we grow, we find that the off the charts service we are known for, starts to slip. We want to attend the closings carrying the perfect thank you gift.... But you get a sign call on a house where the seller really needs to see some activity.... And you don't go. Or the phone calls that helped all your clients de-stress so well, are fewer and farther between. They think they are still better than most agents and great with people but when they are honest, they acknowledge that service levels have slipped. In the leaner years they were the best. Now that they are a mini-monster real estate agent, service is pretty good.

When you get a referral, you need to be available right now. You have asked this person for years to give you a referral and you better handle it quickly and professionally. If you are too busy to do it fast, they will realize that you have gotten big enough you don't really need their referrals.

The alternative for some is to have a system, a team, that can pick up where you need. It assures that anyone who comes through your system, gets a fabulous experience and will thank the person that referred them to you. Sometimes, as we feel our service and thus our reputation, slip, it might be time to build a small team.

Build a Saleable Asset

One of the problems in this industry, is that after we spend years building a business, we just walk away from it at the end. Most companies you can sell when it is time for you to move on. I know we hear of people trying to in effect sell their database to a different agent, but that usually ends up having almost zero value. I don't know a lot of people that feel the same warm and fuzzy when they get the call that says "You know how great it was working with Julie when you bought your house. Remember what a great, really personal relationship you developed with Julie? Well I bought her database and since your last name begins with an A, I am calling you this week to let you know that I am now your Realtor for life and all future commissions will be going through me… So do you have kids?"

I hear it doesn't always work so well. If you build a large team that has the ability to carry on without you, then you have a saleable asset. If you build one such that you only manage things, you are just one step away from hiring a manager and you just collect checks or sell the whole thing.

Two Common Fears

At times I am sure that building a team makes complete sense. So why doesn't every moderately successful agent, build a team? I have heard many reasons but mostly they boil down to:
- Not being able to let go because, of course, nobody can do it as well as you do.
- Fear of taking on the responsibility of making payroll. Can you really afford it?

It can be scary. If you teach your new assistant how you would like things handled when they arise and what your expectations are and then get out of their way, you might find that you are easily replaced in those functions.

And of course, it is scary knowing that you are taking on an expense in order to grow. I mean what if you have a soft month??? Ahhhhh...

Just know that every single team leader I talked to about it, laughs. They were all nervous about the money end of the decision. Most, by the 2nd month, chuckled at their fear. It changed from taking on the additional salary as an expense to an investment that has paid off handsomely. Most wished they'd hired someone earlier.

You will have a bigger business that can afford to pay someone because you will now have more time, to do what you do best. Focus on the things that make you so valuable. Just pass off some of the duties to people you manage. They will have your high standards because you will have taught them.

Teams: Common Mistakes

Not all teams succeed. Hmmmm, those darn humans. Here are some reasons they fail:

#1—Hiring the wrong person. I recommend that you have them take one of the personality profiles to make sure they are a fit. Some use the disc personality profile. I also like the Taylor Protocol which is free on their website. Do not hire someone because they are just like you. You don't need a mini-me.

Monsters

Your first hire is an administrative assistant. That person is different than you. You are looking for someone with different strengths. They will need to enjoy doing the things that are not your favorite or are less valuable.

Do not be weak when it comes to firing someone. If you are asking yourself the question if someone needs to go, the answer is often already yes. If you have to stop and ask yourself then there is a reason and get it over with. An unproductive or grumpy team member will sabotage your efforts to grow immensely.

Do not share some one with another agent in your office. Bad idea. Find someone who can only work part time and you will be better off than sharing.

Stay away from your best friend usually.

#2---Build infrastructure before more growth. If you are overwhelmed with your business and you bring on a buyer's agent as your first hire, you will be more overwhelmed, not less. You will have more business to process than before. That is why you would usually hire an administrative assistant first. Teach them how to handle that side of things and then continue to grow by adding agents, if you choose. Build your infrastructure first and then add agents or personal business, to fill that infrastructure's time.

#3---Don't micro manage. You need to empower your employees. Let them see that you will back them in their decisions. Lead them the direction you want to go and make sure they see themselves as being part of something good. Something that is going to grow and that they are an intricate part of that growth. The best team leaders I met with, loved helping to develop their team members. They really wanted them to contribute more and to be paid more. Cool….

Teams: Common Mistakes

#4---Don't be a tight wad. Be willing to pay a bit more than your competition. That little extra is worth so much in value. You want your team members to feel appreciated and to stay forever. Turn over and re-training is a lot of work. I would also give everybody a promotion and a new title….. Well at least the title. Really, I would not use the term assistant. Rather, office manager, client care supervisor, buyer specialist etc.

Buy Gary Keller's book the Millionaire Real Estate Agent. Read the One Minute Manager, by Ken Blanchard & Spencer Johnson. Find ways to compliment their work.
Ask them what they think are good ideas and suggestions. Give them a huge bonus if they give you a referral. Help them feel vested in your company. When you shift from salesperson to team leader you are building a company.

Database Building Tip

I have always felt that the easies and most fun real estate careers, are reserved for those that work almost exclusively with their database and the referrals from their database..

I have always felt that agents should not have weekly or monthly listing or sales goals. We can not control when we make a sale and so quite often, no matter how hard we work, we fail. We did not meet our goal. Seemed like a good week but we failed to meet our goal. If our goals are activities that we can control, then we are in control of our weekly, monthly and career success.

The number one goal every week until you have a huge database, is to add to your database. The only 2 questions are, how many per week do you commit to adding and what is the goal for the total size of your client base?

If by Friday night, you have met your goal, what the heck, take the weekend off. If by Saturday night you have not, well you'll be working Sunday. You can control the number of people that you meet and thus put into your database. I suggest a number of at least 5/week to assure that by the end of the year, you have made significant progress.

The total number depends on you and your market. I think 500, is a good number. I got to 500 and then slowly weeded out the worst as I added new. I know agents that have 1,500 in their database but most of those only get mailing touches.

One of the best ways to build a large database quickly is to hold open house in new construction. Not just on Sunday, but a lot. Everyone in the county gets a kick out of strolling through and seeing what is new in building. They know they aren't disturbing anyone because the home is vacant. They want to see the pretty houses and get ideas or just dream. They love to see the new

Database Building Tip

building materials and designs. In addition, all of the neighbors will decide on a nice night to go for a stroll and stop and take a look. They feel safe because when they walk in and the Realtor pounces on them, they can say " I'm just a neighbor and not looking to move."

Perfect. What if your goal was to NOT SELL A HOUSE? Then you feel fabulous inside. You are a perfect fit. They aren't buying and you are not selling. What if you knew you will sell an occasional home but that your goal was to add 5 or 10 people a week to your database? You will get more traffic in a new construction subdivision, than any other open house. Most agents hate them because they meet all sorts of lookie loos. They think it is a waste of time. Hmmm, let me think, if you just added 5 people a week to your database, that is about… let me see…. 5 times.. mumble, mumble,,, carry the 1… Wow, not bad for one year of sitting in a place that you could use as your office. A spot that would give you some sales, and allow you to add 250 people to your database. 250 people, that know of you as a Realtor and agreed to receive real estate info, from you.

The best part is that we have a situation that allows us to have a relaxed introduction. They aren't buying. You're not selling. You can relax and be yourself and have fun with it. Remember the part about people work with the Realtor that they LIKE, trust and are thinking of at the time they need one? What a great way to be seen as a likable and successful agent. Some of those neighbors will come by several times and see the progress of their favorites. You will recognize them and be able to show them around in a non-threatening manner.

Here is what I do. I have fun with them and just try and create an enjoyable showing. I give the kids a noogie, show the mom what is new in kitchen designs and start a conversation with dad about the sports team that is on the t-shirt he is wearing.

Monsters

Script

When they are about to leave I say, " I know that now is not your time to move but when your time comes, do you have someone you call your Realtor?" If they say no, I say "Well, here is what I do. When I meet someone that I **think I would enjoy working with when their time comes,** I mail them something from time to time about the market and when you are considering a move, I would be honored to interview for the job as your agent. Is that OK?" Most say sure. I then ask for their name and mailing address. If they then say, here is my email address, I say "Oh, I'm sorry, that's not how I work. You see when I meet someone I would enjoy working with I mail them something from time to time. Would that be OK?" I get almost everyone.

If they respond that they do have someone they call their Realtor, I say " Well, here's what I do. When I meet someone that I know I would enjoy working with when their time comes, I mail them something from time to time and then if someday you are considering a move I would be honored to interview for the job as your **Backup Realtor.**" Is that OK?" People are thinking, "back up Realtor. This guy wants to be my backup Realtor? Whatever, sure." Really, I get almost everyone because we just had a nice time together and they can't imagine why I would want to be the back-up but what the heck? I then stick them in my database and nurture them until their time comes. The best part is that those that say they have a Realtor, by the time they think of moving, that agent is probably out of the business. Many, have gotten so much mail from me that they think I am their agent. Many times I have had someone ask if I remembered when I sold them, their home? Really. I'm telling you gang, one year of sitting open house in new construction, and you have a database that will support you for life. If you sat a lot you could get 10 people a week, just swinging by to look at the new stuff.

Database Building Tip 174

Obviously most of you do not represent a builder. So what. I know of many agents that went to a builder's listing agent and asked if they could hold open. Some of you are skeptical but I know several agents that did this in a different company's listing. They sought out the perfect subdivision that they would like to sit in and pursued that one first. A few of you will be at a company that won't let you do that. Switch companies. They are control freaks. You are in charge of building your business. Many listing agents will love you to help. Do it.

I am not suggesting that you get in to some schedule that takes away your ability to move around as needed. Many subdivisions sit closed up all week. Just tell the listing agent that you would like to be there a lot but can't commit to which hours. You will use it as a second office and come and go. You don't need a furnished anything. Just a table from home and a couple folding chairs.

On a different thought….. if you do this, follow the other new home subdivisions so that you can be the pro, if they want to buy new construction. And… be aware of the used homes that are just a couple minutes form the new construction site. Know which are vacant. Call the owner occupied owners and ask if it works for you to show their home on short notice. Many will let you know if they work days and then you know you can lock up and go show a home if it fits a buyer.

The goal of this program is to meet as many people as possible in a relaxed setting to build your database. However, be ready to sell stuff. Be ready to leave on a moments notice if you get an opportunity. Then come back instead of going to the office.

There is a nice residual to having lots of opens. People that drive by, get used to seeing that you are open odd hours. They will look for your sign sometime when they have time…. Just to walk through…. Not buyers right now…

Boomshackalacka, baby….

Segmentation
(The Wave of the Future)

…… and by "Wave of the Future", I mean that if you do not integrate segmentation into your business relationship development, wave good bye to your future.

We build, nurture and then harvest, from our database. We purposely choose whom we would like to work with, over the years. We target them and develop them, for our whole career. We just need to identify them, let them know that we own them & that they will hear from us forever.(pronounced very slowly)

…foooooreeeeeevvvverrrrrrrrr)

They now, are our database, CRM or book of business, as you choose.

In other places, I talk about identifying, building and harvesting. That is all the easy part. The hardest for most of us, is to "Nurture." We all know the successful Realtor that knows everybody, and is always in an animated conversation with somebody. She loves people and remembers their dog's name and their aunt Susie in Minnesota, now don't you know, eh. He starts up a conversation everywhere. She doesn't even prospect. He goes to the dog park with his mangy little terrier and comes away with a listing, from someone, he just met.

That does not describe me. When I started developing my future clients, into a database, I would call to keep in touch and nurture them. The conversation usually went something like this:

Segmentation

Bob: Dial...dial.... Ring........
Potential A+ client for life prospect: Hello
Bob: Hello John, this is Bob Bloom
Potential A+ client for life prospect: Well hi Bob, great to hear from you. How are you?
Bob: Fabulous, and how are you and Jill doing?
Potential A+ client for life prospect: Both real good, thanks.
Bob: Great, and how are the kids doing?
Potential A+ client for life prospect: Good Bob.....
Bob: Good... good....
Bob: So good, glad to hear you guys are good. How's work going?
Potential A+ client for life prospect: Good, real good.
Bob: Oh, good.
Potential A+ client for life prospect: .... and so, how are your kids?
Bob: Good. Yeah, they are both doing good...
Bob: Thanks for asking.
Potential A+ client for life prospect: Uhm, so uh....
Bob: I didn't want to take a lot of your time just glad you are good.
Potential A+ client for life prospect: Good, good..
Bob: Well it was good to talk to you,.... Oh by the way, do you happen to know anybody that is thinking of moving?
Potential A+ client for life prospect: Boy, nobody comes to mind at the moment.
Bob: Well if you ever think of anybody, would you call me?
Potential A+ client for life prospect: Absolutely. That would be good.
Bob: Good, good. Thank you.
Potential A+ client for life prospect: Good enough. Bye Bob.

Potential A+ client for life prospect: Hmmmmmm...
Potential A+ client for life prospect's wife: Who was that honey?

Monsters

Potential A+ client for life prospect: Realtor Bob.
Potential A+ client for life prospect's wife: Great. I love that guy. What did he want.
Potential A+ client for life prospect: I'm not sure. It was really weird. I guess he was just asking for a referral or something. It wasn't a very good conversation.

Two Months Later

Bob: Dial….Dial…..Ring….
Potential A+ client for life prospect: Oh no……

Ring….Ring….Ring…..

Potential A+ client for life prospect's wife: Honey, if you are busy, do you want me to get that?
Potential A+ client for life prospect:

**NOOOOOOOO.
IT'S BAAAHHHHHHBBBB!!!**

    The problem for many database developers, is that it is way too awkward, to call people for years, to nurture them. For me, it was impossible to continually call someone, when I had no purpose in calling.
    Yes, we can mail them monthly, which works for some %, but another %, needs the call. I don't have to pretend, that I invented the fact, that an in-person visit, has greater effect, than a newsletter. Right after the in-person in value, is a phone call and a real conversation.
    I just can't do it. I can not comfortably call, and have a warm and endearing conversation, unless I have a purpose to call. I

Segmentation 178

knew that was a huge weakness for me, and I had to overcome it. You can imagine, how well that worked. A nervous, uncomfortable, sales guy, that is not great at small talk, putting extra pressure on himself, to be witty and clever. I won't type out that conversation for you but believe me, it was much shorter.

The key for me in having a chance, to have "Potential A+ Client for life prospect," look forward to hearing from me when I called, was if I had something to say. Hmmmmmmmm. Wow, something like a purpose for the conversation that gave me direction.

My only hope was to segment my database. I just had to categorize them into segments that I can identify and call up as needed. WWDD. What Would Dale Do? Good old Dale Carnegie, might have said, that it would be very interesting to my clients, if I called and talked to them, about what they think, is very interesting.

(....AHA....) The question became: What do they think is interesting? I was clueless. I was clueless, because I had not yet segmented my database. Now it is easy.

In my CRM (database system), I have searchable categories such as gardener, Oregon Duck fan, music or wine lover, fisherman or hunter, loves to cook, Christian, atheist, loves dogs, golfer, has kids, sports nut, runner, has a boat, but that is a different purpose...connection to Oklahoma, connection to Colorado, big basketball fan etc.

Now I say " Hi Fred this is Bob Bloom. I was thinking of you today and just had to call. I heard on the radio, the annual yard and garden show is this weekend and it made me think of you and your incredibly beautiful yard. Are you going to the show?'

.....or I say " Hey Fred, I was thinking about you today and just had to call, how bout them Ducks, eh. Big game this weekend"

....or I say "I was thinking of you today and just had to call. March Madness starts tomorrow and I am clueless. I know you probably already have all the winners picked and maybe you

Monsters

could give me some insight, before I look stupid and fill out my bracket."

....Or I say "I was thinking of you today and just had to call. Do I remember that you were from Oklahoma? And she will say yes and I will say, I was concerned when I heard about the tornadoes. It looked really bad. Do you have any family that was affected?"

.....or "Hey I know you love to go shoot up those elk, are you going this weekend?"

....or "I was thinking of you today because I heard they are having a dog show, out at the coliseum and I know how much you love your pooches."

....or "I just had to call. I saw there is a seminar on gluten free cooking and I thought of you."

....or "Oh my gosh Joe, I saw they have candidates night at the school auditorium and I know you love politics."

....or "Jill, I hope it is OK to call, I saw they are looking for cooks to bring their best sample for a chili cook-off, and when I think of great cooks, girl you are it. That meal you made, me is still in my top 2 all-time favorites. I can't imagine what you could do with chili."

....or "I was thinking of you when I saw the season schedule came out, for the free concert in the park, series. Have you seen it or can I email you a copy?"

....or "I know you are new in town. I just thought of you when I was talking with a friend, about the monthly art crawl downtown. It is a nice way to get to know downtown and meet some people. Have you heard about that yet?"

....or "Jane, I had to call. I heard on the radio about the shooting at XYZ University. Doesn't your daughter go there?"

Segmentation 180

....or "Mary, I was thinking of you today and I just had to call. I know your son's over in the Middle East. Today, on Veteran's Day, I wanted to call and see how he is doing. Thank them for their contribution. Let them know you appreciate them and their child, and share with them, the most meaningful conversation they could have in life. How is their child, whom is in harm's way, doing? They are proud and scared. They will remember that you care.

Not just their kids. If someone has sacrificed for our country, they will love to be acknowledged, on their day. Ask them some light details about their experience. Next time you will know where they served. Build your database of data with each call.

When you get segmented, never again, miss thanking the past and current veterans. That is an easy one.

When I hang up, they are glad that I called. We have further cemented our relationship and they like me, even more. We had a nice, short conversation, about something they want to talk about. Sometimes I ask for a lead and sometimes I don't, but if I do, they know, that is not why I called.

Next time I call, they answer the phone " BOB, HOW ARE YOU?......and are excited to hear from me.

So, how do we do this?

The most important step is, to use a CRM system that allows you to develop your own categories. It has to have the ability for you to develop" unlimited" categories (or segments I call them) of your own.

There is no software currently available that has every category that you need. When you run across someone that graduated from the University of Nebraska or is a quilter, you need to be able to create that category. Then we learn to keep our eyes open for signs and ask pointed questions, that we keep track of the answers.

If we see they have pictures of grandkids, we can easily remember that, when we see an article on how to speak to kids about drugs.

If they have a plant on their desk, I categorize them and then know whom to call, when the yard and garden show comes to town.

If I see a Christian symbol, I am not going to send a "Happy Holidays" card in December. I am going to send a "Merry Christmas" card, because that is one of their segments.

I mention quilter. I recently heard on the radio about the "Quilters Show." I couldn't remember if I had any, but I pulled up "quilter," and found that I apparently, have 2 clients, that are into the whole quilting thing. I called and said " I was thinking of you today...." I'm telling you, they loved me. Two for two, thanked me. One said, that she would try and get me a referral sometime soon, if she could. I believe they both went to the event.

It is not enough to put that information into the remarks section of your database. You need to have software that allows you to create unlimited search fields. The data does you no good, unless you can search for all of those that fit into a category, with one button. The goal is to have a database of clients and future clients, that is way too big, to remember all your quilters.

I don't care what you use, but most CRM software has a pretty small limit on the number of search categories, that you can create. You need a lot. I know ACT allows you to search by any word, so that, works. I have used them. I currently use Realty Juggler and pay $99./year. It does not have the most bells and whistles, which I don't care about, but it lets me build unlimited search fields.

Segmentation

This has no value if you don't train yourself, to look for the things that would be fun or interesting to somebody. Perhaps not you but apparently, somebody. Pay attention to the radio ads for events. Make a habit of checking the entertainment section in the newspaper and local entertainment blogs, to find reasons to call.

Segment your database and your clients will love you. They will look forward to hearing from you, instead of using caller ID, to screen you. There is much talk about relationship selling. In order to build a relationship, you need to go deep.

Find what they find interesting and figure out how to develop that.

Don't Worry... Be Happy

I believe that people choose a real estate agent that they:

Like
Trust
Are easily aware of, when they need one

As a result, we must be professional and relieve their anxiety in order to be **trusted**. We must continue to drip market to all of those that like and trust us, to **be the one they think of** at the time.

That leaves **like**. Would you guess that people prefer to hire someone they like or someone they do not like? Duh.

We can not go in as Mr. Funny Guy. No ne is hiring a comedian at the moment. They need a professional that will get the job done. If they have that confidence that you pass that test, then move to the next level. Let them have fun in their experience. It can be very stressful. We relieve their stress if we are pros and we keep it light. Let their house buying adventure be a dash stressful but mostly enjoyable.

Have fun. People like to have fun. Include a few reasons to laugh. Joke about the process and how crazy it is. After difficult conversations, leave them with a smile. Acknowledge that was the hard part and then find a way to lighten it up as you head out the door. Leave them les stressed and they will remember you with warmer feelings.

Some agents believe they have great value if they are constantly saving their clients from some greater conspiracy that includes everyone else in the transaction. They show their sellers a

Don't Worry... Be Happy

million nightmares and then are the hero. Those poor people come out of that experience emotionally drained. They are not feeling like giving a referral because they would never advise anyone ever move again.

Have your clients be able to tell their friends and family that they enjoyed the process and it went smoothly. Bob handled everything and kept it stress free. He is pretty good and kind of a funny guy.

The bonus benefit is that we get to have fun. It is your life. You can travel through along from one fire to the next or choose to have fun with it. Having fun with it is a lot more fun than not having fun. Life is short. Choose fun. Be a pro and be serious as needed. After the pro stuff, lighten it up and have some fun. That would be fun for you and fun for your clients.

I suggest two approaches:

Give yourself permission to relax a bit. Think of your image more as a calm and relaxed pro with a sense of humor.

Add some humor to your scripts. Find a way to build in a relaxer in the middle of a presentation. Do a post meeting analysis. Take a moment to look back at your appt. and see if you missed an opportunity to add a relaxing moment with a chuckle.

Monsters

Welcome to this chapter.
I'm glad that you made room.
I hope I have ideas for you.
Let's get started, I'm Bob Bloom.

I have so very many thoughts
that I'd like to share.
Not just because I like to talk
but really, cuz I care.

Although I care about you,
I don't about your year.
My interest and my focus
is on building big careers.

This race it is so simple.
You are not the 1st to do this run.
And some of those succeeded.
So, just do what they have done.

And what they did was obvious.
To all it is quite clear.
I can tell you what you need to do.
So listen up you, you'll hear.

Welcome

The 1st trick is quite simple
so, open up your mind.
To have a great last chapter
begin with the end in mind.

Who will all your clients be
from where your income comes?
Will they be executives
or homeless drunken bums?

I recommend you pick a niche
and then that you dominate.
I prefer big fish, small pond
so you're never 2nd rate.

So here's the most important thing
and it begins on your day one.
This job can be a nightmare
or it really can be fun.

In order for it fun to be
and keep the happy face,
the only way that old Bob knows
is through your database.

Monsters

This job it gets much easier
when the sellers all call you.
That happens through the database.
I know these words are true.

You need to do your affirmations
and you need to meditate.
You need to have your weekly goals
and not leave things to fate.

    (N. Dakota accent)
You need to hold your open houses.
That's true, now don't you know?
You're going to have to pay your dues.
That's also true.... Now don't you know?

I recommend you study hard.
Learn something everyday.
This job can truly be the best
but those dues you'll have to pay.

Me, I always loved this job
and the freedom that comes with it.
I never missed a single game,
recital, play or skit.

Welcome

Yes, I worked some crazy hours
but it's better than a job.
I made a decent living
and was allowed to remain, Bob

Please read my words intently
and please do what I say.
It's really not an ego thing.
I'd just really like to help……..O.K.?

Zillow

Allow me to take a moment and talk about the greatest real estate authority on the planet. Zillow...

Maybe it has never come up for you before but in my market, I never need to give a CMA. The sellers are all smarter and much better informed than I am. Old Bob, after doing exhaustive research.... OK.... exhaustive might be a bit of an exaggeration. I never wing it. I do everything I am supposed to do, to make sure I am educated about the current comps and the state of the market. I include average days on the market, number of months inventory available and have analyzed all the similar solds and pendings to make sure I am completely prepared.

However, I find that it really wasn't necessary. 5 minutes after I arrive the seller tells me what his home is worth as figured by Zillow. Why call old Bob when you can get a ZESTIMATE. Aye, yi yi.

I try to tell them that just like county assessed values, sometimes they are pretty close but often I find they are not. But how can I possibly compete with something off the internet. We all know that if it is on the internet, that it is true, right? Especially something that took me 2 hours worth of work and it spits it out instantly. They even have the ability to do that with millions of properties around the country everyday.

I will briefly give you some data that I hope is helpful for you when that comes up in your life.

To Zillow's credit, they don't even put as much stock in their Zestimate, as do most of my clients. They actually publish an error rate after homes close to show how close they were. For example in little markets like San Francisco, Sacramento, Las Vegas and Dallas Fort Worth the month I looked 50% of the estimates were off by 10% +. That's not bad, eh? So for example on a $300,000. Home they are only off by about $30,000. Really, $30,000. Don't you wish the sellers were that forgiving of you. If I am off by $30,000, my clients think I'm an idiot. The same client tells me he knows his value because he has looked it up on Zillow which is that far off 50% of the time.

That same month, the Zestimate was off in similarly unimportant cities like Pittsburgh, Detroit, Chicago, Cincinnati and Cleveland. There the estimate of value as given by Zillow was off by 20% or more approximately 20% of the time. How would that go over if on the same $300,000 home you were only within $60,000. Do you think the seller would care or notice if we said the $300,000 home was worth about $240,000. I don't know but in my market sellers expect a dash better job than that.

Being off 20% is a problem and when Zillow says they are accurate x% of the time is a problem but here is the bigger issue. I read of a house that Zillow said was worth $439,000. After it was listed for $1,350,000 Zillow changed it's Zestimate to $1,200,000 based off of seeing the listing price. When it sold for $1,300,000 they were only off by about 8% when really the month before they showed it as worth 439K or about one third of the sales price. They adjusted their Zestimate after they saw what price it listed for and used that number instead of their estimated value one month earlier to analyze how accurate they are. You probably can't really get into that with every seller or you look like a whiner but internalize it is true and start to accumulate real stories from real listings and sales in your area to have printed out and ready to show them when needed.

Having Said That….

In today's world I believe the real estate pro will include Zillow in his or her preparation while doing a CMA. Not because I am suggesting that you use that number but I believe you should assume that there is a very good chance that the seller would have

Monsters

seen that number. You should pro-actively bring it up and address it. You should let your sellers know that you too looked at and considered Zillow and took into account some additional data to come up with a more accurate price valuation.

To find Zillow's accuracy analysis you have to look close but it is there. Go to Zillow.com and then from the home page scroll all the way down to the bottom where you see the categories: "About" "Zestimates" "Jobs" and "Help." You know that area across the bottom of every website that no one looks at. Hit the Zestimate button at the bottom of the page not the Zestimate spot in the middle of the page.

When you go to that screen you will find a tab that you can click on called "How accurate is the Zestimate." There they have a chart that shows you the current month and what they believe their accuracy is. It updates monthly but is something you can print out and have as part of your presentation to make sure your sellers understand that it was one more tool that you use. It is the least reliable so you also actually, did your job and came up with a real number.

I would also like to point out that a potential client that has already been on Zillow and gotten an estimate of what their home is worth is probably a little farther along in the mental shift to moving than many of those that have not. Do not pooh pooh it. Let them know that you too have been to Zillow as part of your homework but that you also have additional info. Treat those people seriously because they probably are serious.

We also need to be aware that potential buyers for your listings also often check out the value on Zillow to confirm what the "REAL VALUE" is. You are going to lose buyers that believe that is the number even when it is way off. I have seen homes that were more than $100,000 off on a $300,000 price range. They were $100,000 low and we have lost buyers because they assumed that number was accurate. More often you

Zillow 192

won't know this has happened because the potential buyer never looks at the home. They believe it is priced too high. So when it is low you should have your seller go in and try and amend the data and dispute the accuracy so that at least your thoughts are on file. Also have the seller tell them the list price.

OK, so here is the thing, I know that you know that Zillow is not always accurate. You didn't need me to tell you that. What I am suggesting is that you can either go in with the "huh uh,, big no fair. My number is better than theirs" approach or be proactive. I believe that it is important that you be prepared to include the Zillow data when you are on a listing presentation because even if they don't mention it, the seller may have been on their site. You should show them the Zestimate proactively as one of the many things you analyzed and without making it a big deal. You should have in your tool kit a printout of Zillow's accuracy chart so that you have 3rd party (meaning Zillow themselves) dispute the reliability of those numbers. When it is appropriate have your seller try and address the issue when they are way low in case a buyer looks at it as well.

As an additional note: Many homeowners don't realize that Zillow is a lead generation business that captures them and sells their name to me. They need to be good enough to attract a million of them and some of you. They don't need to be accurate, all the time.

Luxury Homes

Many of us dream of owning the Luxury market. Average sale price about $2,000,000. in some markets. Higher in others. Keep up your same pace of sales per year and Boomshackalacke, baby. Life is good.

I learned two concepts from the Monsters about being a Luxury specialist:

First: Building a large Luxury focused business, is as easy as any other niche or area you might choose to farm or pursue. It is the same process as if it were the $200,000 price range. If you do the activities, you will succeed in that market.

Second: It requires focus. You need to be focusing on the development of that niche and not dabble in it. Dabbling in the luxury end is hard. Choosing it and focusing on it, increases your odds of success, greatly.

It is a little different animal and if you have a track record of sales in that market, you gain the credibility to have a huge advantage over the real estate agent that mostly sells in a lower price range. Commit to it so that when you get an opportunity, you are educated and experienced in the upper end. That makes you the obvious choice instead of one of the choices.

This category is no different than any other. You just target it, develop a game plan and do it.

First thing you need to do is commit to get the National Association of Realtors Luxury Home Specialist designation. I know, you can't actually get it until you have closed a couple, but take the class now. Be able to tell people that you have the education part out of the way and if they would just work with you then you would qualify for the designation…. Or at least have the knowledge from the class. Commit to that as the first step. Any

Luxury

real estate agent that is half serious about being a Luxury Queen or King, would do this.

You can't with sincerity say to the seller that you are the best agent for the luxury listing when your competitors' business cards say, they are the Accredited Luxury Experts and your business card says "agent."

It is much easier to get a listing if you have a buyer. Having a buyer allows you to show property and become educated on the market. It allows you to call any FSBO that might be out there. It gives you credibility. Whether you are currently working with a buyer in that price range or you have closed one recently that you can talk about, it can be used as an entry point.

So how do you get a buyer? Find a listing that you can advertise. Either an agent at your company, a FSBO or a builder in that price range. Someone will let you run an ad.

Though open houses are a different animal in this arena, look for two things: One, find a vacant home in this price range and offer to sit open house all sorts of different hours. Not just Sunday. Make it your office on and off at different times throughout the week. Do the same thing that you would do for any open house and meet the neighbors, send out postcards ahead of time and be prepared to add value when someone comes through.

Second: find a builder that is building in this price range. Most builders are begging for open houses and constantly hear how they don't work. They do work if done correctly. What a great way to get next to a builder but more importantly, if you meet a buyer every two weeks and can start to dip your toe into the deep waters of big bucks, it is well worth it. Remember, doing opens is not your goal but rather phase one of building a monster career. So run ads and do opens, as if you already own that market segment.

I recommend that you preview every listing that is in your target price range and has been on the market longer than 90 days. It will allow you to learn the market and it will position you to call on them as an expired. Sellers hate it when they have been on the market and then get a cajillion calls the day they expire, only to hear repeatedly, "I could sell your home." All they can think about is why didn't you. You didn't even show it.

Soooo, make sure you have been inside of the homes that might expire. Do not lie and pretend you have a buyer, if you do not. It is OK to tell them that you are trying to focus on this segment and just want to preview the home. A lot of these homes expire once or so. If you have earned the right to call them by having seen their home, you will stand apart from the average "expired workers." How much better is the conversation when you say " You have a fabulous home. I loved your backyard and there is no way to describe your master bedroom adequately. Someone has to get inside of your home to appreciate it." So preview every home and work the expired listings.

You are going to think I am crazy but I have heard it repeatedly. The rich are no different than the rest of us. Most of them are self-made and they started at the bottom. Many worked their tails off to get where they are and thus RESPECT THE AGENT THAT IS NOT TOO COOL FOR SCHOOL AND IS WILLING TO WORK HIS OR HER BUTT OFF and do the basics.

You know where I am headed, door knocking. Phoning and Knocking and Mailing, oh my…

Yes, yes, there might be the occasional butler that screens you and there are some gates that get in the way sometimes, but not always. No one door knocks in that neighborhood.

Stand out by doing the same things you would do anywhere. Find an open to hold and door knock around it. Follow the new listings and when there is one, treat it as if it was yours. Send out postcards and DOOR KNOCK around it. When a home goes pending or closes, treat it as if it were your listing and do all the things the listing agent is not going to do.

Luxury 196

Send another round of mailings and door knock around the home to update the neighbors you met earlier.

No One Else is Doing This...

It won't take much to be seen as a hard worker Most of the agents currently embedded in that market, think they are above all the basics.

Most of the homeowners that scratched and clawed their way to the top, will appreciate and respect that you are willing to do the same. In fact, don't be shocked if from time to time you hear them say "You remind me of me, when I was getting started."

Just let them know that you have chosen to specialize in homes in their price range and are the hardest working Realtor they will meet.

One thing else about door knocking, make sure you are the expert. Before you go knock, take a few minutes and do a mini CMA for that neighborhood. They might say yeah, what did the home around the corner just sell for. You better know. So check what just sold and what is active. Look like someone that knows the market.

Next, meet the gatekeepers. There are profes-sionals that currently serve that market. The estate attorneys, financial advisors, accountants etc., that know these homeowners and are asked who they recommend as a Realtor. Get next to them.

It is a methodic process but meet them and let them know that you are targeting that market. Tell them that you would appreciate their help. This same group can become your partners later when you have a co-op invitation, open house. Market to this group differently. Send updated stats and items of interest. Keep them updated as to

Monsters

your success so they know you have carved out a niche. When possible, look for an excuse to take them to lunch or a ballgame. Look for opportunities to refer someone to them, to help build their business.

Find a commercial real estate broker that you can refer back and forth to. He/she meets clients that need to sell their residence and you will meet people that own commercial real estate. Both of you will need someone to refer them to.

The next step, is to become part of "that" community. Live there if you can. If you can't afford it, don't. But go where they go. It might be time that you start seeking out and attending the charity functions in your community. You don't have to be the biggest auction buyer of the night. Start to mingle and meet the owners of luxury homes. Find causes that you are passionate about and volunteer. Many volunteers are the wealthy and have time on their hands.

If you are a golfer, step up and join the club. If you play tennis, do it at the right location. You will find that the wealthy are craving the chance to talk about real estate. They want to do it with someone that doesn't accidentally squeal when they say 6 million. So hang out where they are.

It is not impossible to have a large business that is mostly in the Luxury Home segment. It does take focus and a commitment to keep with it. When you have made it, you will chuckle. It is not nearly as crowded at the top as it is trying to get a listing from the $250,000 FSBO.

After you have the listing, things are a bit different than the starter home. You might have to be present when other agents show the home. You might not get a chance to hold a normal open. (though, you might)

Two types of opens you might get are the Broker Open, which I highly encourage in this price range and a by-invitation open for locals of notoriety, owners of other similar priced homes, neighbors and friends of the seller.

Luxury

Make it nice and serve champagne. If it is too expensive for you at this point, include a marketing partner like a high end jeweler that is displaying some nice pieces or one of those financial planners, estate attorneys etc. Have some nice hors d'oeuvres and make it fun. You might find a high-end caterer that would like the exposure for free. Maybe line the driveway with cars from the local antique car club or have an art exhibit at the homes.

I have also heard of having a tour of several high end homes on the same day by-invitation only. Make some buzz around it and invite all the interesting and well-healed folks in town.

It is important in this market segment that you develop a personal brand. Put some time into a logo and slogan that you can keep forever while working in this price range. Remember it is important that you set yourself apart. Do it with class and showcase your brand. There are companies that create coffee table books that are personalized with your brand. Send them out to those that are in your database..

Some monster agents drop off a pre-listing book to their home or office the day before their listing appointment. Same as you should do at a lower price range. However, make this one with a hard bound leather cover. Make it professional and classy. It might cost $25.00-$50,00 but helps you stand out and gives the seller an outline, of what they will see tomorrow from you.

You should also expect to spend a little money on a professional photographer. One that will take some drone videos as well as stills.

Commit to set aside as much as you can from your first commission and set up a long term printed, marketing campaign. Now if you can afford it, as soon as possible in any case, establish an image of you in the local paper or those real estate magazines in the grocery store. Make it consistent that your marketing is mostly high-end homes. These are very valuable to show to your new listing prospects. It shows that you are month in and month out, an Active Luxury Expert. Once again, advertise anybody's home or listing that will let you.

Internalize that the sales process is the same and the need for practicing your scripts is even greater. Did you get that? You still need to use your scripts and would be wise to practice them before you are standing in front of a person with a 10 million dollar listing. They are pros, probably. They certainly have had many pros present opportunities to them. Do not wing it. They expect you to have a script, to be professional in your job. They are used to seeing the best and the best polish their words ahead of time. They are used to seeing visuals, charts graphs etc., so use them.

Lastly, make sure you manage client expectations. Just like I now want to do with you....It is important to understand, these homes might take a bit longer to sell and it is harder to figure an exact list price. You and they, need to be flexible and be willing to adjust as needed. Listen to the feedback, as the market speaks to you.

It is not impossible to have a large business that is mostly in the Luxury Home segment. It does take focus and a commitment to keep with it. When you have made it, you will chuckle. It is not nearly as crowded at the top as it is trying to get a listing from the $250,000 FSBO.

Be Like the Salmon
Swim Upstream

We love referrals. Those of us that have a business model different than holding open house for the rest of our career, need referrals.

Elsewhere, I talk about how important it is to thank the referrer. We know that. If we thank them it encourages them to repeat the referring behavior. If we do not thank them, they are less likely to do so. That is a fact. I think some guy named Pavlov first talked about that.

Since that is true, the goal is to look for reasons to thank our referrers. The more reasons we can find to thank them, the more likely they are to refer us. Cool.

One way to do that is to swim upstream. The salmon is your role model. When we get a referral do not just thank the referrer.... Swim upstream. Thank the person that referred the referrer to you. When we can call someone that has helped our business grow and surprise them...it leaves an impact.

Calling someone to let them know that the person they referred to you, has now referred someone else to you, reminds them of what a large impact their actions can have. We remind them that their prior actions are still
helping us and we acknowledge and thank them. That will make them once more aware of opportunities they run across that might get them thanked again. Our subconscious likes to be acknowledged for our worth and value. It likes to be thanked.

Swim upstream as far as you can. Thank them all and spread the love. Those actins will come back and spawn for you again in the spring.

Snow Day

We all need to have some phone communications with the people in our database that we are nurturing. It is difficult but necessary. It is difficult for two reasons. First: Small talk is hard if you have no purpose to your call. Without a clear direction for the call to head to, it can be uncomfortable. Second: People have busy lives and when we call they may be in the middle of 13 things all at once or may be sipping tea in the garden. We have no way of knowing which state of mind they will be in. The harried mother or relaxing prospect.

Here is one small solution. Be prepared and excited for the next big snowstorm. The bigger and more traffic crippling, the better. When that happens all of your clients have an unexpected day at home with nowhere to go. They will be home and they are not busy doing things that they planned days in advance. They are all home and probably not in the middle of anything more pressing than a game of Monopoly.

In addition, there is an easy flow to a conversation whenever there is some weather issue. The T.V. has non-stop coverage and everyone you visit has an easy topic that is interesting and current. It is not just a cliché'. People do like to talk about the weather.

When I say be prepared, I mean have access to your database wherever you get stuck at. Prepare some "Snow Day Activities" for your clients that have kids. When you call, offer to email it to them. Have fun indoor activities and some creative outside snow play time. I have included some samples of them. Get some free images off of pixabay.com to use along with the tips.

Snow Day

Decide ahead of time how you will best take advantage of the God given gift of the Snow day. Turn what could have been an unproductive day into one of the most productive. Touch in with a plethora of your clients and potential clients in one day.... They will be home waiting for your call....

Boomshackalacka, baby....

String 'em up   (No, not the kids)
Take a piece of paper and fold it diagonally. Then half it once or twice more. Now cut designs into the paper and unfold to find the perfect snowflake you have created. String them up around the house or on the Christmas tree if it is that time of year.

String 'em up #2
Make an extra large bowl of popcorn. While enjoying the snack. String some up and then hang it outside of your window for the birds to eat.

Watch out for the yellow snow..........
Take your average snowball and put it in a cup. Add your favorite Italian soda flavoring mix or juice for a home made snow cone.

Shake it up baby now....... I
It's easy to make your own snow globe. Use waterproof glue to secure a plastic figurine to the bottom of the

inside of a jar. Throw in some glitter and add boiled water, after it cools. Screw the lid on tight and walla...

Camp the great Indoors

Just because your schedule or the weather prohibits you from getting out to your favorite camp site doesn't mean you can't go camping. If you have a pop-up or a dome tent, set it up inside. If you don't, take some blankets or plastic and drape it over the couch or dining room table. Cook smores in the micro. Turn off the lights and tell stories by candle or flashlight.

Ahhhhhh... I was soooo cute...

Take some time and go through your old photos and scan them into a digital file. It will be fun to see them, help preserve them and entertaining to create a scrapbook.

You can teach an old dog a new trick...

The old saying is not true. Old dogs can still learn. How fun to be able to show off a new trick with your pet to your friends or family. Google "dog tricks" and how to teach them. Not as hard as you think. Don't let anyone know you are working on it and surprise them with Wonder Dog.

Snow Day

Careful! Don't trip over the couch…
Bored? Nothing going on? Try re-arranging a room or two in your home. It doesn't have to be forever. Just stretch yourself for a week or two and try a whole new look.

Tutor yourself…….
There are a ton of free classes you can take online. Spend time surfing the net to find something that interests you & go for it.

Hey, you little squirt………
Fill up a few spray bottles with different colored water. Let the kids loose in the snow to create their own masterpiece. Snow art.

Ice… Ice… baby………..
Use food coloring to create several colors of ice cubes. Now go hide them under the snow in a designated area. You can give clues or just let the kids search like an Easter egg hunt.

No two alike… Really??
Place a black piece of paper in the freezer till it gets cold. Take it outside and catch some snowflakes on it. Use a magnifying glass to inspect the snowflakes.
They really are all different..

Sasquatch, eh Watson………
After a fresh snowfall, go outside and look for fresh tracks. Try and guess what made them. Google local birds and small animals to confirm their footprint..

Come on baby light my fire………….
Try hiding a flashlight inside of a snowman or under a bit of snow and watch it shine through.

Have a snowball fight or…

Prospecting 101

I found that the monsters all had specific scripts to ask for referrals. They were all very comfortable with the words they chose to use and have a few to be able to easily pull from. Even more interesting, is that most of them mentioned that they just plain ask for more referrals than most people. They have their systems built around giving great service and having specific times that the request a referral. It is built in to that system. They always ask for a referral at… whatever… event and they always use the same words.

That is huge. We need to have and practice our scripts. However, we should understand that the goal is to ask more. If we ask a lot we will get better and better with our words of choice. Analyze your business and find the times that you need to be aware to ask for referrals. They might be:

On every first appointment
At the inspection
On the third phone call
The day after their offer is accepted
Every January
At lunch appointments
Etc.

The first rule of prospecting is to ask more times in life than other real estate agents. You need to be able to do that in a way that is comfortable for you so you don't feel that you are annoying people. That requires for you to choose the words that work best for you and to practice them.

There are two parts to that equation: The transition going from out of the blue to give me business. That is the hardest part for many agents. How do I get from here, to there. That is covered elsewhere.

After your transition, you need to be comfortable with 3 questions:

Who Do You Know?

When are you Moving?

Will You Refer Me?

Who do you know…..

Which one of your friends is the most likely to move next?

OR...

Who do you know that might be thinking of moving soon?

OR...

I know you aren't going anywhere but which of your friends is most likely to move next? May I contact them?

When are you moving???

When do you think you will move next?

OR...

How much longer do you plan on staying in your home? May I contact you then/

Will you refer me??
If one of your friends or neighbors wanted to move, whom would you recommend to them as a Realtor? How do I become that person?

Practice your version of those 3 questions until they flow comfortably without a thought or any nervousness. Now, go find people to say them to.

Monsters

I recommend that if you are serious about growing your business, that you time block a major portion of the morning to prospecting by phone. It is when you are fresh and thus you are more effective. Do it before the day drags down your energy level. It is most effective if you give yourself 30-45 minutes at the beginning of the day to check your email, make a phone call and make sure your day is organized. Then close the door to the world and crawl into the womb-like warm and cozy place of phone prospecting.

Really. if you are a professional, most people are not shocked if you do your job once in awhile and call. They expect you to check in on your potential client and or friend. Set aside at least one full hour to call your sphere, the day's expired listings, especially if you recognize it as a home you have shown, or any new FSBO's that showed up on Craigslist. Just make sure that you have prepared whom to call before your hour starts. Make sure that your committed time is focused and not wasted on spacing around craigslist. Decide ahead of time, who you will call during that hour. If there is an event that is going on, call who would have interest in that event.

Baseball's Greatest

Today I'm going to talk about
baseballs greatest batters.
Why so, you ask.
I say, cuz it matters.

The greatest ones we talk about.
And about them we tell the truth.
Me, I think the greatest were
 Hank Aaron and Babe Ruth.

We know them for their big stick
and the infamous homerun.
We know they were committed
and off the field had fun.

But I never hear us talk about
 they usually would fail.
Strike and strike and strike again
but that's not in the tale.

All the greatest players
they'd try and try and try.
It's the way to be a slugger
commit to swing or die.

Old babe would mostly strike out
but we conveniently forget
cuz then he'd hit a homerun
and we would win our bet.

Monsters

The superstars will tell you
they are not always great.
But their strike outs never stopped them
from stepping back up to the plate.

The same applies to you and me
if we choose to face our fear.
We may hear a lot of booing
but in the end the cheer.

If Hank and Babe had given up
and gone and got a job,
the sport would not have been the same
fans memories they'd rob.

But because they never gave it up
but swung and swung and swung,
we know them as the greatest
their praises we have sung.

That's all I really want to say
about those famous batters.
Why I do I talk about this?
You know, cuz it matters.

Pain or Pleasure

I might disappoint some percentage of you, as you find out this chapter is not some 50 Shades of Grey thing. Come on. I'm a business coach. I can't be writing about ……. Well, you know.

As you read about my script concepts you will see a repeating theme. Somewhere in the script we tend to remind our clients about their dream. Their dream is their current Big Why…. for many and at least the motivation for moving, for the rest. Selling your home is not fun. The stress of prepping and showing and negotiating and then….. you get to box up your life's stuff and have Uncle Fred with two beers under his belt, unload them.

There has to be a pretty good reason as to why someone would go through that. The task is so formidable for some that they never move. I believe they use words like, I will never do that again.

The key to helping them is to keep things moving and fairly stress free. Sometimes I believe the best of us get paid so much because that is their goal. A stress-free, smooth transaction. In order to reduce stress and anxiety, help them let go of some of the details. Maybe you do them a huge favor if you help them accept an offer that was lower than they hoped for. We said we would help them. They need to move in order for us to be successful in helping them.

One of the best ways to do this is by keeping them focused on their goal. If we do that, it gets them where they really want to be. Remind them of their dream and be specific. By the time life is over, few of us will be deeply impacted by the $10,000 we hoped to get and didn't on that one house…. Honey, which house was that now? No, our life is determined by if we got there and did so without going through hell.

Monsters

It is important to ask a few more questions upfront. Don't just take the listing because you can. It might be a referral or past client where you have total control. Slow down and find out what is at the heart of wanting to move. Something big inside is going on, to want change. Change is hard so it must be big.

People move for one of two reasons. They are moving away from some pain or are hoping to move towards some pleasure. It is either away from bad or towards good. Pain or pleasure.

Find theirs.

People move away from the pain of:
  Barking dogs
  Lousy neighbors
  Bad schools
  Crime
  Small bedrooms
  Tiny yards
  Traffic noise
  Snow, rain, heat or cold
  Racism
  In-laws and Uncle Fred
  Bad influences
  Bad Memories
  The Big City

Pain or Pleasure

People move towards the pleasure of:
Better Homes
Bigger Yards
New Opportunities
Better Schools
Safer Neighborhoods
To be Closer to Family
The Country
Sound of the Water
Back Home Where They Grew Up
Different Weather
The Perfect Place to Retire

    The main reason we need to know their specific dream is so that we are able to remind them. It is part of our job to know their why and remind them, if it helps them to accomplish that.

    The second reason is because we are more successful when we keep people in their "comfort zone." They are more relaxed and make decisions easier, when they feel comfortable. Part of that "comfort zone" conversation looks at the words that your client uses. The monsters listen to the exact words that their clients use and then they use those words when speaking with them.

    Our vocabulary is very personal and meaningful to each of us. Our words come to us from years of experiences. Some of those words are emotionally charged. Could be a positive charge. Could be a negative charge. When we speak in the same vocabulary, their mind relaxes. When they have to stop and interpret or use different than their usual words, their brain works harder and that puts them in a state of unease. That applies across the board. Sometimes we use real estate agent words. Sometimes our words are too professional. Yes, they are smart enough to know the meaning of our words but those are not their comfort words.

Monsters

If someone shows you their yard do not later tell them you love their lawn. You love their yard. If they call the great room a family room, family room it is. Use their words, so that it flows for them.

The words that we use, matter.

The third reason why need to now their true moving "why," is that most people make decisions from an emotional level. Much of what we do in life is not necessarily logical. Love, marriage, kids and most home purchases, are coming from an emotional need. A need, towards pleasure or away from pain.

When people are looking at legal documents and talking about the math of this sale, they are in a very logical state of mind. Most people become frozen when that happens. If they usually make decisions that are justified in logic but are completely emotional, this is scary. This is different and they should slow down. It just doesn't feel as comfortable as needed.

If you are professional enough to bring the conversation back into their emotional side, they will thank you. They appreciate it if they get back to their decision making "comfort zone" and yes, we do love this house, Bob. We bring them back to their dream to shift their thinking style from logical to emotional.

We obviously do not say, "This will get you to your dream." That has no impact. Duh, Bob. Be specific. It might be similar to:

Guys I know this is not everything WE hoped to get but it does give us everything we need and the timing would be good, so you can get to your grandkids before school starts. We can keep trying and hopefully net a little more but it is pretty tight to make it by September first. I know how important that is.

OR...

Except for price this is a pretty clean offer. I'm on your side, I'd like to see us get a little more out of this but I feel I should say something right now. You hired me to help you and I will represent you anyway you want and continue to do my best. But you hired me to help you and I think I am supposed to speak up and remind you two ,why you are doing this. You told me the most important thing was to get to the country and I would like to get you there before it is too late to plant a garden this year. You did not tell me the most important thing was to net $14,300 more. This isn't fun and I know the only reason you guys are doing this whole deal, is because you want to get to a quiet place with no neighbors and a big garden. This offer accomplishes that. So I think we are supposed to slow down and consider this one strongly.

OR...

As the Realtor in the room, may I say something? Thank you. I want you to know that this is not a sales thing. I really like you guys and you hired me to be the professional. I feel I have to speak up and you might not like it but sheesh that is why you hired me. I know how important it is for you to get to a part of the country that has a healthier job market. Of course part of that, is that we need to get you as much as possible out of this home. But I think we are supposed to look closely at this offer because it does do that. It is a pretty quick close and they seem qualified. We need to get you on the road so that you can start being paid close to what you are worth again. We don't need to feel rushed but guys every week or month that we stay is another week or month away from doing that. You hired me to get you to a place where you can live with family and get your career back on track. That is pretty valuable and I am supposed to make sure that "I" remember, what your main goal is.

Combo Bombo to Success

I have entitled this chapter, "The combo bombo to Success." I'm not sure if any of you will ever read this because of that crazy title. Hmmmm, I guess that means I am talking to myself again.... Whoa does that mean I need years of therapy??? Just in case anyone is still reading.... that was a rhetorical question... I do.

The "Combo Bombo" is a complete business model that will not only bring you success rapidly, it will build a solid foundation for your business for years to come. For at least one agent this was the path to Monster status.

What is the combo? I have always felt that in order to make money in this business it is important to help buyers buy homes. It also seems like we need to help sellers, sell their home. Go figure, eh?

Just as important, if you choose to still be in the business in 2-3 years, I believe it is very important to start to build your database. That way you don't have to work as hard in the future. Am I off here?

I am going to propose to you a business model that will help you combine a survival income for the present while developing a monster future.

Sooo, here is the plan. First, I suggest that you commit to holding open house several days per week. Find vacant homes that you can use to hold open. Commit that you will use the vacant home as your office and go there everyday and work from them. Have a table and chair in your car so that you can be comfortable. Take with you whatever work you would have done at the office. Will you get a new client everyday. Heck no. Not even close. Will

Combo Bombo 218

you pick up at least one real buyer every week. Absolutely. If your expectations are to just sell 4 homes a month from your open houses, you will be thrilled with your results. By holding open so often, you will hone your skills and be very good at capturing potential clients' names and numbers.

Some of us hate open houses because of the whole Rodney Dangerfield deal. We think of ourselves as professionals and know that we can help people with their moving needs. You probably know that you are a better Realtor than the one that many will end up working with and yet people treat us like old Rodney. They won't give us their name and number or they lie to us or even worse they insult us by saying they will give us their email. More about that later but if I am at an open house and someone wants to give me just their email address because it is the best way to reach them, I tell them no thanks. That's not the way I work.

What if you could say to them " This morning I talked to a potential client that has not listed their home yet but wants to sell. I believe they will be in your price range. I hope to meet them tonight or tomorrow. After I have more information, would you like me to call you so that you can be the **first person** to see this home before it goes into multiple?

Wow…. Now they will be excited to say… please take our phone number. **Everybody wants to be the first** person to see a great home that just hit the market.

So here is the key: you need to develop a FSBO program in conjunction with the open house program.

So how do we be different and thus more effective working the FSBO's's, than everybody else? Easy. Do the Combo Bombo deal.

Imagine this approach. You call up a FSBO that is priced at $300,000 and tell them that you are going to be holding open house today in a $300,000 home that is in their area. You hope to meet some buyers in their price range today. Ask them if their home is still available and if it is OK if you try and show it to a potential client, if you get one.

Monsters

Almost all of them will say yes. Do not try and get the listing. Ask them if it is OK if you drive by their home before your open house so you can honestly say that you have seen the outside. (duh, is it OK to drive by your home?... you might get a yes on that one) And then do it. Really do drive by.

Then tell them the address of the home you are going to hold open and the hours you expect to be there. FSBO's get lied to all the time by the idiot agents. It will be really refreshing to them to have someone who is obviously not just calling to get a listing. Someone that actually has buyers for their type of home and someone who apparently works hard.... In their price range and area.

Then, after the open house, call the FSBOback and tell them that you did drive by their home. Point out something about their home that let's them know you really did drive by and let them know that you really liked the looks of their home from the outside. Now let them know that you did meet a potential buyer if that is true and you would like to preview their home to see if it is a fit. If you did not meet a buyer, call them back and let them know you drove by their home and love it but did not meet a buyer today. Let them know that you are holding open house again tomorrow and will call them tomorrow if you meet a hot one. Maybe ask to preview it anyway or maybe wait until tomorrow and call back to let them know you really did hold open again and now you did meet a buyer.

So what does this do. You will be the most honorable Realtor they talked to. People like to work with people they trust. You will show them that you are the hardest working agent in your county. How many Realtors won't even hold open house on the weekend and this hard working nut case is holding open on Tuesday and then again on Wed. People like to work with hard working agents and they have all heard about (and if they haven't you are going to tell them) about the agents whose business model is to work FSBO's. They're just listing agents that just want to get a listing and throw

Combo Bombo

it into multiple and not actually even try to show it themselves. They will see you as an agent that works hard, that will actually try and show their home yourself, is consistent and honest.

So that is steps one and two of "the bombo" I said I would show you how to get more buyers. If you use an open house as your office 5 days a week, you will have buyers at all times. If you actively work FSBO's and show that you are different than every other agent they meet, you will get some listings.

Now for the third leg of this program. The part about building for the future. Do what you are supposed to do when you hold an open house. Knock on the neighbor's doors. If your open home is vacant. You are OK to leave the home and door knock around it. If you see someone pull up, tell them you have to go. Meet the neighbors and let them know that you are the neighborhood specialist and that you will be holding open the next few days and feel free to stop by. Ask them if they have any questions about the market that you could answer for them. If they seem like nice people, let them know that as the area specialist you will drop something in the mail to them about their area from time to time. Then when you go back to your open, stop and look them up and enter their name and address into your database. You can usually get their phone number online. Then set them up on an 8x8 or 5x5 but mail them something before the day is over.

Treat them as one of your own. If you hold an open at the same location a few times, go and knock on their door again sometime. Whenever that home goes pending, go back to everybody again and let them know that it is pending and ask if they know anyone else that might be thinking of moving. I am telling you guys, if they have met you once or twice and you seem like a nice person, if they now see you as a bit of a neighborhood specialist and they definitely see you as the hardest working Realtor in town because they don't see anybody else holding open on Wed or Thursday and if they are now receiving mail from you…. you own them. Batta boom batta bing… the Combo Bombo….

Buyers, sellers and building a huge database faster than you ever could have done by just adding clients one at a time.
So here are some key thoughts.

One: hold open in vacant homes only. That way if you get a hot buyer, you can close up and go show them another home that is close by. Some sellers won't care if you come and go even if it occupied but vacant is nice.

Two: if you don't have a vacant listing use one from one of the other agents in your office.

Three: read my open house chapters as to how best to capture the buyers. It will involve you having data that you can share with that client about other homes in the area and how to prepare for that.

Four: have a million signs out. People will drive by and see your signs a couple days in a row and be looking forward to hoping you are there the next day, when they have time to stop. Bring them from a distance not just from around the corner.

Five: work the FSBO daily and let them know you are at open again or you are showing their price range again. Let them know that you would work this hard for them as well, if they choose to use an agent. Ask them to stop by and see the open because it is their competition and will give you a chance to visit with them. They probably won't come but they will be impressed with you.

Six: practice your open house scripts. If you are going to be the king or queen of open houses, make sure you become good at capturing clients.

Combo Bombo

Seven: commit to using this strategy to build your database and set goals as to how many people per week minimum you will add to the database. It needs to be at least 5. That is easy to do if you are meeting buyers and neighbors. If you only did that you would have an additional 250 people in your database in one year. Then you might keep doing this because it is so easy or you may have enough folks to stop and just work your database. That is the goal. Build your database while selling a bunch of houses and representing a bunch of sellers along the way.

Eight: I told you I would talk more about the whole email address deal. Here is what I believe. In order to keep a healthy mental attitude in this business, we have to reduce the amount of abuse we take. There is nothing worse than leaving an open and being way up because we got two new clients and then after three weeks of emailing them homes, we find they won't even call us or email back. We have proven to them that we are the same as every other agent that emails them homes and we have taught them, we have no real value. Now we crash as we learn that we really have nothing and have wasted our time. Be strong enough to not take their email address if you don't also get their phone number. By being firm we will get a higher percent of phone numbers and we also will not set ourselves up for the crash when we figure out that they never had any intention of working with us.

There you go. A business model that gets you more buyers, a great excuse to interact with FSBO's and a logical, database building component.

Boomshackalacka, baby....

That is a Combo Bombo...

The Fast Eat the Slow

One of the things the monsters all understand is that the fast eat the slow, in this business. The reason many of them first got an assistant was because they were too buried to respond quickly to a new lead. They were too busy to tell the sign call that they need to see the inside and they will be there in five minutes. They were finding that they have about a minute to respond to prospects that dialed one of their 800 listing information messages. If you wait five minutes they can't even remember the house and are not impressed. They are more likely to respond, "What took you so long. I called 4.7 minutes ago."

I have personally had way too many lost pieces of business because I assumed there was no or less, urgency. I get a call from an old client that tells me he wants to move in the spring and could we meet sometime in about a month or two to plan for that. My next call is them telling me how happy I will be for them because of the great home they bought. They saw an open house and it was perfect. Aren't I happy for them?

I have had clients tell me there is no rush. We're just starting to think about moving. Of course they told their sister who told her best friend Realtor Julie, who took a little more of an excited and aggressive approach with this, her new listing that could have been mine.

I talk elsewhere about the reticular activator. It is real. It is our filter that lets in and blocks out information to protect our little pea brains. Once they start to think about moving, their reticular activator goes on fire. It makes them aware of every for sale sign in the country. They all of a sudden remember 18 people that they know who are real estate agents. They pick up on every real estate conversation because their awareness level is heightened.

Meantime, you are at back at the ranch contemplating how many months you should wait before you go see them.

Some of us have gotten a sign call and were very professional. We got their info and then committed to email them listings. Wow, that really makes you stand out.... they probably don't have 15 agents emailing them the same stuff, which they can find online without us.

What is more effective is to convince the buyer they need to see the inside and you are on the way. One of the best ways to nurture your database is to show your own listing. These are one of your current most likely sources of referrals, so show your own listings whenever there is a chance. They love you when you can. That is one of seller's main complaints. The listing agent never showed it personally. Take the chance to please your seller and pick up a new client. If you meet them in person it increases your odds geometrically.

Some of us have been guilty of meeting a prospect in an open house and committing to get them their info in the morning. Then they drove around the corner and met an agent that closed up her vacant open house and took them over to the perfect home and they made an offer. If we are going to sit in an open house, be ready to close it up and go show a home if you meet a great buyer. If you don't show urgency they will drive around the corner and find an agent that is hungrier. Show urgency.

It applies everywhere. It is a true balancing act. We need to time block and not be deterred from our chosen activities easily. We do not go herky jerky through life responding to outside stimuli. We time block and nurture our database. We also understand that opportunities are often fleeting. Even if it is your best and happiest client. The same client that has referred you 4 times. The client that said no hurry but I am thinking about buying a..... That client will bump into a dozen of you, once they start thinking about it. Be first in order to cement your position.

Now You See It...
Now You Really See it

I remember my first sales job. They taught me my presentation on a flip chart. I hated that. I looked like the rookie that I was, as I flipped along. My prospect would casually and humorously follow along while I tried to be interesting, while flipping.

They did this for two reasons. One: I was an idiot and their only hope to get their message delivered in a cognizant, fashion was to have me read what they wanted me to say. Second: they knew that no matter how badly I sucked, if the client saw the pretty pictures they would get it. They really didn't need me to be able to speak an entire intelligent sentence. Just be able to read and let the pictures speak for me.

What they knew was that;

83% of people learn best through sight

11% of people learn best through hearing

Hmmmm.... Even more interesting is that the MONSTER real estate agents know the same thing. The exact person that you would think is way beyond any cutesy flip chart... uses visuals in his/her presentation.

The pros have all the visuals with them. They know that their presentation's impact will be greater if they use them. Because the Monsters analyze their closing rations constantly, They know the odds of a sale are improved when they visually back up their words. Words are enough sometimes. However, if 83% of people best learn with visuals, only a fool would not include them.

If your personality allows you to pull out and follow a flipchart, do so. Some monsters do exactly that. it allows them to control the message and the sequence of their points they want to make.

If you are not able to do that, as I am not, have the visuals that you might pull out ready and accessible. As you visit through your presentation, stop at least once and pull out a visual that reiterates the point you are speaking. Literally stop and say. "Hang on let me show you something I saw that is interesting" and then pull out the visual. Even if you don't use them in a presentation format, refer to a few and pull them out as needed. Know exactly how to quickly reach each and make it look spontaneous. You will know exactly when you will use each and how to best access it quickly.

Sometimes we don't need to use them. Sometimes we do need to use them. It never hurts our professionalism if we pull out materials that make our point for us visually. Sometimes it helps. It never hurts…. Hmmmm….

Monsters

Noun:
1. A closed plane curve consisting of all points at a given distance from a point within it called the center. Equation: X x X + Y x Y = R x R
2. The portion of a plane bounded by such curve
3. Any circular or ring like object, formation, or arrangement:

OR....

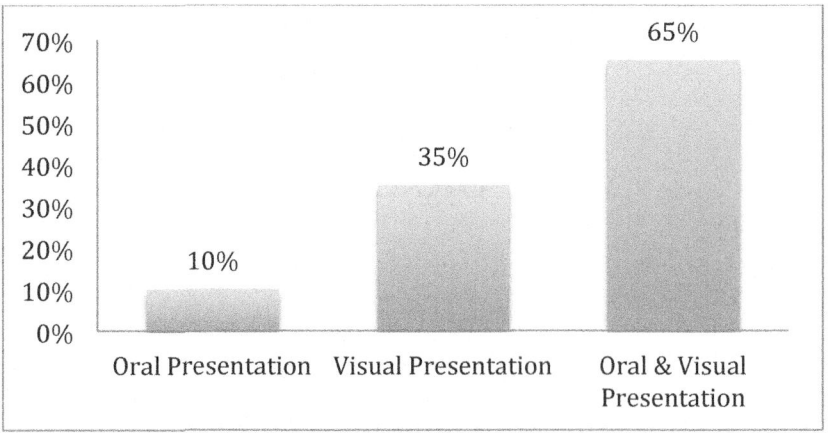

**OSHA studies show that 3 days after your presentation,
 a combined delivery
  creates a 65% recall.**

Normal or Buyers Market Listing Tip

As I write this book, the current chapter seems silly. We are in the hottest market of life. There are bidding wars and races to be first. With that comes downward pressure on fees. Sellers are pretty sure that your 90 day marketing program, won't be needed.

However, because I am old, I know this too shall pass. We will have normal markets, buyer's markets and seller's markets in the future. That I know.

Skip this for now but remember me when the cycle turns.

When we chase listings we need to differentiate ourselves. We have lots of competition. In the county of 300,00 people that I live in, there approximately 300,126 licensed real estate agents. We have competition from their Aunt Betty, the local guy that has farmed them a long time, the past agent they used before and the big team on the radio.

We need to be able to tell them besides a cheaper fee, why would they choose you. I don't think having access to multiple listing works anymore.

#1 Agent in the County for…..

I was never the top agent in my county, if we are counting total sales volume. However, I told listing prospects that I was the #1 real estate agent. I told them I was the #1 favorite listing agent for all of the other real estate agents in town. I let them know that every Realtor around loved showing my listings more than other agent's listings. If they could only show one listing today, they are all hoping that it is mine.

Normal Market

I let my prospects know that I would try and sell the home and I have all the marketing and internet stuff etc. that we all now have. The difference is that I take $500.00 out of my fee and have a drawing when the home closes. All real estate agents that showed the home for me, are in the drawing. I email them a thank you for showing and remind them that they are in the drawing. After recording, they all get another email showing them who won. Many know each other and can hassle each other over this house's winner. It is quite fun and sometimes agents might even send you a text from the showing, letting you know they are in and send the old smiley face.

We do not give a bonus to the selling agent. That is a waste. The buyer chooses whether or not to buy the home, not the real estate agent. All the real estate agent can do is get them there. Our goal is to get as many of them there as possible.

If the seller wants maximum exposure, let them know that there are so many agents out there that you will never meet all the buyers. The best way to make sure every buyer sees your home, is to make sure every Realtor wants to show it.

When we differentiate ourselves, we give the seller justification to choose us. It is easier to explain to Uncle Fred that they would have chosen him except this one agent they met, gets the most showings.

Keep copies of your emails to the Realtors to show them. When an agent sends you the perfect "Love Email" after they win, ask them if you may use that as a testimonial. That is huge. If you can collect emails from the top agents in town stating that they can't wait to show your next listing….

Boomshackalacka, baby.

P.S. Don't be a tightwad. This will get you a ton of listings if you work the FSBO's. If your price range is higher, give $1,000 in the drawing.

Monsters

Warren says....

My roots are in Nebraska. If you are from there, most likely either you, or your mom or grandma, own one or more shares of Berkshire Hathaway. We all know where Mr. B., (only his closest Nebraska friends use that term) lived through much of his life. He was right there, on the busy street with no fence, around his home....and.... if you own a share, or you can drug your mama to sleep and steal hers, you go to the Big Event. Berkshire Hathaway rents out the CenturyLink Center to holds its annual shareholders meeting. That, is a sight to see and worth the price of stock, for admission.

Upwards of 50,000 people will come and go, at the open house, referred to as, the "Woodstock for Capitalists."

All of the companies that are under Warren Buffet's umbrella, show their wares. They display the newest, latest, greatest and probably your favorite item, and sell to the stockholders at great savings. It is more like a festival of ice cream, cowboy boots, candy, furniture and insurance.

Inside the arena, people come and go. Up on stage, sits Mr. Buffet and vice chairman, Charlie Munger. They sit in big comfortable chairs and have a fireside-type chat, with their shareholders/fans. Folks come up to one of the microphones and may ask anything they choose, no restrictions, and the 2 try to answer everyone. They laugh, are relaxed and very thoughtful, in their attitude and responses. Fabulous party, with live entertainment. Sometimes they sit up there for eight hours, if people keep asking questions. Just a lunch break to mingle and back. They are so human and yet so brilliant, that it is a joy to see.

One year I saw a man ask about the effect on the company, if an earthquake took out California. They laughed and joked about it being too warm down there anyway and glad we invested heavily in Nevada. They then explained their diversification strategies and insurances that would handle it just fine..... Surprise.

Warren Says...

I saw a tribe of Native Americans come up to the microphone. They were protesting the company's ownership of an electrical dam, that blocked their native rivers. They wanted the dams removed. They were allowed to come up and chant and sing their traditional songs and then say their peace, because the tribe owned a share of stock. The gentlemen on stage were respectful and sincere. (The native Americans have won almost all of those battles against Berkshire Hathaway, at this point. In each the company, not only had to pay to remove their own asset that had been government sanctioned, but in addition, make restoration to the tribes. Costs ran over 30 million per dam and then they lost the revenue stream of those power plants. (I'll bet old Warren choked on that peace pipe)

And then there was the little girl that shyly, approached the microphone. She looked to be about 13 years of age and looked very nervous. At first her voice cracked and she had to start again. She spoke so softly that the coliseum got eerily quiet. Everyone in the aisles, stopped. She squeaked, " Mr. Buffet, sir, as long as I have memory, my mom has worked really hard to take care of my brother and me. I feel so lucky that she cares so much and we're both doing well in school, but she works two jobs and I know she gets tired sometimes. Sir, if you could give me one piece of advice, to help me make sure that someday, I am in a financial position to return that favor, for my mom, what would it be?

Warren leans forward in his chair and looks her right in the eye. It felt as if 49,999 of us, were completely blocked out, and he was talking directly to her and to her alone. Warren says, " You, are a very brave young lady. The key to your success, will be in your ability to choose your friends, wisely. For you see, we drift in the direction, of the company we keep. The best advice I can give you, is to be very careful with whom you choose to associate."

Same Words but Why

I would like to visit about **saying thank you**, to our clients. The, when, why and how, of saying thank you, in a professional setting.

Now come back here, don't tune this out yet. This is not going to be what you think. You may think you don't need to hear this, because your mama taught you all about having good manners. I am going to take a different approach and reference some interesting research.

Why

Let's start with why. This is the most obvious part of the equation. Our mama's taught us, that it is good manners, to say please and thank you, and you don't want to disappoint your mama now, do you? Huh??? OOPS... my bad. I joke, yet I don't. We know down deep, because that is how we were taught, that thanking people, is the right thing to do. If we don't say thank you, we are actually going against our grain. If we told our mama, we would say thank you and we don't, we are not treating ourselves with great integrity…..the infamous, slippery slope.

But there is much more to it than that. People like to be appreciated. Some days it feels like there are approximately 2.6 million salespeople in the county of 250,000 residents that I live in. I don't care if you live in Wahoo, Nebraska or New York City, there are probably more salesmen and women, than there are folks that live there. People have a lot of choices and they know it.

But, they have chosen you to work with. I believe it is imperative, to acknowledge that, to your clients... and I am not talking about "thank you" as you are leaving. I believe you should, at some point in the conversation, stop and make a real point of acknowledging, that you realize they have many choices and you

Same Words but Why...

really appreciate their business. I tell them that I am honored to represent them, because that is true.

The same applies to thanking people that give us referrals. If you would like them to give you another referral sometime, you need to reinforce their behavior, which encourages them, to repeat it. Why do we thank people.

Why

Because it is the right thing to do and because it reinforces their behavior, so that it feels good to them, to repeat the behavior.

Adam M. Grant & Francesco Gino published their data on this segment of gratitude, in The Journal of Personality and Social Psychology. In their studies, they asked people for help and thanked some and did not thank others. They found that the participants, who were thanked, were more willing to provide further assistance. Indeed, the effect of 'thank you,' was quite substantial: while only 32% of participants, who received a follow up request for assistance without having been thanked, did so, the number of people willing to help went up to 66%, if they had received a simple thank you, previously. That's a 100% increase in willingness to help, just for doing what your mama told you to.

Many of us live in a referral based business. When we are fortunate enough to identify people that are referrers, we develop that relationship, thank them and make it feel good for them to help us.

When we are fortunate enough to receive a freebie, develop a relationship with that referrer, thank them and make it feel good for them, to help you..

The third reason that we should say thank you, is that it makes us feel good. Literally. In the relatively new field of positive psychology research, gratitude is strongly and consistently linked to greater happiness. Expressing gratitude helps people feel positive emotions, relish good experiences, improve their health, deal with adversity, and build strong relationships. This is not one of those deals where I explain to how that works. Let's just go with the research and say "cool."

Studies were done by psychologists, Robert A. Emmons from the University of California, Davis & Michael McCullough from the University of Miami and Martin Seligmann from the University of Pennsylvania.

In summary their research shows, if people either wrote thank you notes, or kept a gratitude journal, in which they wrote what they were grateful for daily, they reported a 25% higher happiness level, had fewer visits to the doctor, were more optimistic, exercised more, had better and longer sleep and reported an improvement in their personal relationships. That's a lot of good stuff for just saying thanks, or by daily, contemplating your good fortune.

What is really interesting to a "show me" kind of guy, like old B-O-B, is that not only do we now have anecdotal information, reported by the test subjects, but researchers have measured and found proof of the effect of having an attitude of gratitude. (hmmmm, I like that… attitude of gratitude) They found physical evidence, that supported their theories, with a variance in cortisol levels, reduced stress, heart rate variabilities and even increased activity in the prefrontal cortex.

Did you get that? There is anecdotal as well as measurable, scientific evidence that shows that if we learn to say thank you and if we write thank you notes and/or create a daily gratitude journal, we will be healthier, happier and have an improvement in our personal relationships. Cool…. And sooo easy.

When

When: Immediately and often. Really. When we get a referral, we don't wait until we get the listing to thank them. We give the referrer/buyer the immediate gratification, of thanking them immediately and letting them know we appreciate it (I say honored). We then reinforce it by thanking them and updating them on the progress. Don't over do it, but people love to get an update when the the referred client finds a great one subject to inspection and then closes on their new home. Make it fun for them as well. That's how we reinforce the behavior and encourage them to do it again, sometime. We make them feel appreciated.

In today's cell phone addicted world, it is a great idea to text or email from your cell, a thank you for your time and nice to meet you and I will get back to you as soon as I get the info I told you about…moments after you leave a client. Second: There are mobile apps such as thankyoupro and thankyounote that you might check out, that will assist in that.

Third: I believe that we all should carry in our briefcase, thank you notes, so that we can pull over right after an appointment and write it and drop it in the mail on the way back to the office. In most communities, there are mail drop boxes that have a last pick up between 4:00 and 5:00 P.M., and if we get it in the mail by then, your client will receive it the next day. Readers, listen to me…. Clients are not surprised if they get a thank you note… though most sales people don't ever make the effort… but they are shocked and impressed if they get it in the mail less than 24 hours after they talked to you. It will really set you apart. Yes. Some cities are 2 day, but the point is the same. Get it in a mailbox, before the last pickup for an extra bump.

How

How: An in person Thank You is best. People appreciate you making the effort to come see them. Also most people love to get mail…. No, not junk mail, but most of us, get very few hand written letters anymore and it really stands out, when we do. Write them a personalized, thank you note.

To infuse your thank you with a dash of cleverness, try saying "mahalo" or perhaps "mahalo nui loa," which is the Hawaiian equivalent of thank you very much. Or Maybe "arigato" [ah-ree-gah-taw], which is thank you, in Japanese, merci or merci beaucoup to add a French flair or bring out your German side with a Danke [dahng-kuh]. Not a big deal, but it does add a bit of flair and makes the thank you more memorable, by speaking in a French accent and exaggerating your pronunciations.

Many Realtors, give a gift at closing. Often, it is always the same for every client, such as some sort of gift basket. Personally, I like the personal touches better. How about if you took a picture of your clients in front of their new home, while they are at the inspection or on your last visit, at the property and then create "We're moving" postcards, that they can mail out to their friends. (maybe you include a, brought to you by Realtor Bob, note preprinted on the card)

I also like taking that same picture of your clients and creating, their own personalized postage stamp. How cool is that? Especially, if they didn't know you could do that. For $21.00 you can get 20 legal, first class stamps….. that have their photo on it. Go to : zazzle.com., photostamps.com or pictureitpostage.com. to create them. Why not be unique and give them something that they have never bought for themselves.

In our market, we have one of the largest Cutco salesmen in the country. He built his business around engraving Realtors names, on really nice knives and then the agents give them, as thank you gifts. I have heard that people really like them, because

Same Words but Why...

of their high quality and the Realtors get to keep their name front and center, every time they use them.

I have known agents that find a local artist, preferably one of your clients, that draws a penciled picture of their new home.

There is a website called reagentgifts.com that sells customized packing tape. Not a big thank you gift but pretty cool and has your name on it.

One of the things that makes a gift memorable, is if it is something that uniquely fits the recipient. What are their interests? If your client is a gardener, go buy a really cool ornamental shrub. Make sure it is something that stays small, so that they have many choices as to where to put it. If your client is known to enjoy a bottle of wine or a brewpub beer, you can buy cases of wine that have your own label on them, or many brewpubs sell growlers, that you can stick your personalized label on. Match their interest with your gift. If your client has kids, consider buying annual passes to the local zoo.

If your client is a big sports fan, consider buying them a flag of their alma mater, that they can hang outside, on game day. You will find on the internet companies that make custom doormats, with the logo or design of your choice.

You get the idea. Skip the one size fits all, thank you gift and take a moment, to think of something that will have some staying power and let's them know that you made the effort, to get something they would find special.

Because, we are commission folks, it is OK to be a bit self-serving, so long as our heart is in the right place. Soooo, maybe you would send a thank you gift to someone's office. If you do, include helium filled balloons or flowers because they attract attention and the other people in the office, will ask them what the special occasion is. Since we want to make it easy for our clients to remember to give us referrals, why not attract attention from people that might say, I'm thinking of moving too. Perhaps you would include some of your business cards, with the gift and balloons.

My last thought on saying thank you is that whatever format you choose, is to make sure that you come from a place of sincerity. When in person, don't rush it. Stop and let them know that the comment is from your heart and not a knee jerk reaction thing, you say to everyone. If it is a gift, make it special. Daily, write down in a gratitude journal, what you are grateful for. Remember, saying thank you and being grateful, will have a huge positive impact on your life. It will bring you things you will be grateful for and want to say thank you for.

Hmmmm, what a tangled web we weave.

Reticular Activator

The whole reticular activator conversation, is a very recent phenomena, but is widely accepted as an easy way to create a conversation about receiving referrals, from our clients. The conversation goes something like this:

Have you ever noticed how when you are pregnant, that all of a sudden, you are aware of pregnant ladies everywhere? Or bought a unique car that you really liked, but as soon as you drove it off the lot, you saw them everywhere? That is the part of the brain they call the reticular activator.

You then explain, how your business is the same way and now that they are buying this, they are going to be aware of people everywhere, wanting to buy the same thing. Does anybody come to mind that might be doing this, as we speak? If so, may I call them. If not, then I often find as soon as we leave or tomorrow at work, you will spot someone and think of me. Sometime, when we talk, may I ask you if you thought of anybody, after I left?

Whenever we are asking for business, we need our client to be in a "Happy Place." To do that, we need them to be in their comfort zone, so do not turn into the Little Professor and educate them about "Reticular Activator." We use examples that fit their lives. If they have young kids, we talk pregnancy. If they have a new van, we talk vans. If they have an ugly dog, well, you know. If they are regular folks, maybe we use the term "Subconscious" instead of "Reticular Activator."

What about me?

In addition, I would like to have you think about the reticular activator, from a different view. Don't just teach your client to look for opportunity, for you. Create a greater awareness in yourself, so that you recognize and then develop, more opportunities.

Understand the same thing, that we tell our clients will happen to them, happens to us. The reticular activator, is the foundation to many brainstorming techniques. The recommendation, is to start a separate file, where you capture all ideas about one specific BIG THING. Decide a worthy goal to achieve and come back and forth to it, constantly. Add notes and develop past ideas. Have a to do list and time projections. Enter crazy, creative ideas and thoughts on how to implement your idea.

The act of collecting all of the thoughts that our mind will throw at us, on a specific goal, sets our reticular activator, on fire. There is a huge compound effect, as the mind goes all sorts of directions and is given permission to create. The more times we come back to our notes and add to them, the greater awareness our "Reticular Activator" has. It will automatically spot possibilities all around the subject, you have chosen. When we hit these "on fire" stages, we need to carry something with us, to capture ideas immediately. Paper and pen, your phone, tablet etc. I have a small hand held recorder that takes one button to push and I am capturing that fabulous thought, before it is gone. I never miss a thought. I must have a dozen of those recorders and one is always close by.

This brainstorming style, is essential in developing:
--- a new business model
--- career development
--- creating new marketing
--- choosing a new direction or niche

Look at it often and continually capture, organize and analyze all ideas.

The key, is to do at least one of the "to do" items, or add to the notes, every day. Doesn't matter how small, but you continually collect and are constantly taking baby steps or bigger, in that direction daily.

The main concept of this chapter is to point out that the whole "Reticular Activator" deal is not just a closing tool. It is a closing tool, because it is real. If that is true, then we need to also develop it, within ourselves and not just ask our clients to do so.

We need to teach our clients to look for opportunity for us and we need to train ourselves to use it to its fullest advantage to direct our personal focus.

What we focus on, is what we find. Now you know why.

The Reticular Activator 201

Now that you get that part, let me back up and tell, as Paul would say, the rest of the story….. the reticular activator is actually a filter system.

There is too much data, that comes our direction and it would overwhelm our brains, if we had to categorize and remember, each item. We are not able to absorb it all. When we have brought a topic to the forefront of our lives, our reticular activator recognizes that topic, out of the flood of information, and allows that data to come to the forefront of our thoughts. If it is information that might be relevant to us, it allows it in. It tries to filter out the rest…. An attempt at sanity.

Focus on your Big Why and ideas will come from everywhere as your activator lets you see it all.

2 most Important Questions 2 Improve your Business

There are a million good ideas that, if we implemented into our lives, would have a positive impact. They go from a small, non-event thing, to a major commitment and lifestyle change. In this section, let's simplify things and look at two sentences, if asked and answered honestly, could be as impactful to your lives, as any major commitment.

Because I am a big fan of under promise and over deliver, let me say that, these two questions can take you from struggling, to a monster salesperson….. or #1 to untouchable King…and that is an under promise…..

Don't change anything else in your life. Just respond to these two questions. They not only will change your career, but have a short term, immediate impact, on your business as well….. er… uh… if you choose to ACT on the new information that is. Hmmmm, maybe I should do a chapter on how thoughts are not enough. It still takes action and commitment…. Nah... No one would want to read about that.

Question #1
What should I do more of, which would have the biggest impact, on my business?

Because it has the highest value
Because you are the best at it
Most Important long-range activity
Most Urgent short term for income
New niche development
Because you are the only one to do it
Productive activity that I avoid
Productive thing I did when I was new

Question #2
What should I do less of, that would have the greatest positive impact, on my business or life?

Takes a lot of my time
Drains my energy
Activity or client that wastes my time
Easily replace me. "Anyone can do it" activities
Low dollar return for the activity
Someone else is better. Pay them or learn it.
Someone less expensive than me, can do it.
An addiction that holds me back
A bad influence: person or place

Folks, this is easy.
You don't have to do this everyday, but this is not one and done. Incorporate the concept into your business model, to make major decisions and small corrections. I suggest you make it part of your weekly Board Meeting, with yourself. Think Big Picture. If you choose to be headed to the ideal career, what one thing do you need to start doing and what one thing do you need to stop doing, to keep on track or to adjust to, "on track."

Remember, the question was, the one thing, that would have the greatest impact. Greatest impact. Do not cheat and add or subtract something that is a good idea, and a lot easier to do, but that is not the one biggest thing that would have the greatest impact… unless #2 or #3, is all you can handle now, then do that.

This does not alone, guarantee monster businesses, but should give you the biggest bang for the buck and immediate results. Really, sit down and without all the data, that many great,

Monsters

long-term plans have attached to them, just decide what will give you an immediate increase in performance or results (both long and short term goals) Do it this week.

The key is to commit, to doing whatever those two things are. You probably already know that you could be more successful if you...... Decide that it is now, so obvious, that you really should do it. Choose integrity to yourself.

As everyone's favorite, Forrest, would say "And that's all I have to say about that."

Give m **a BOOYAH for simple** and a

BOOMSHACKALACKA for relevant.

The End.

Made in United States
North Haven, CT
27 March 2025